# Essential Flash™ 4
# for Web Professionals

ISBN 0-13-014327-8

9 780130 143273

90000

## Other Books in the Series

- *Essential CSS & DHTML for Web Professionals*
  Dan Livingston and Micah Brown

- *Essential JavaScript™ for Web Professionals*
  Dan Barrett, Dan Livingston, and Micah Brown

- *Essential Perl 5 for Web Professionals*
  Micah Brown, Chris Bellew, and Dan Livingston

- *Essential Photoshop® 5 for Web Professionals*
  Brad Eigen, Dan Livingston, and Micah Brown

## Coming soon. . .

- *Essential ASP for Web Professionals*

- *Essential JSP for Web Professionals*

# Essential Flash 4 for Web Professionals

Lynn Kyle

Prentice Hall PTR
Upper Saddle River, NJ 07458
www.phptr.com

*Library of Congress Cataloging-in-Publication Data*

Kyle, Lynn.
   Essential Flash 4 for Web professionals / Lynn Kyle.
      p. cm. -- (The Prentice Hall essential Web professionals series)
   ISBN 0-13-014327-8 (pbk.)
   1. Flash (Computer file) 2. Multimedia systems. 3. Web sites--Design.
   4. Computer animation. I. Title. II. Series.
   QA76.575.K95    1999
   006.6'96 21--dc21                      99-044865
                                         CIP

Editorial/Production Supervision: Benchmark Productions, Inc.
Acquisitions Editor: Karen McLean
Cover Design Director: Jerry Votta
Cover Design: Scott Weiss
Cover Illustration: Jean Francois Podevin, from *The Stock Illustration Source, Vol. 5*
Manufacturing Manager: Alexis R. Heydt
Editorial Assistant: Michael Fredette
Marketing Manager: Kate Hargett
Project Coordinator: Anne Trowbridge

 © 2000 Prentice Hall PTR
Prentice-Hall, Inc.
Upper Saddle River, NJ 07458

Interior photographs used by permission of MJ Wilson Photography.

Prentice Hall books are widely used by corporations and government agencies for
training, marketing, and resale.

The publisher offers discounts on this book when ordered in bulk quantities.
For more information, contact: Corporate Sales Department, Phone: 800-382-3419;
Fax: 201-236-7141; E-mail: corpsales@prenhall.com; or write: Prentice Hall P TR,
Corp. Sales Dept., One Lake Street, Upper Saddle River, NJ 07458.

Printed in the United States of America

10 9 8 7 6 5 4 3 2

ISBN 0-13-014327-8

Prentice-Hall International (UK) Limited, *London*
Prentice-Hall of Australia Pty. Limited, *Sydney*
Prentice-Hall Canada Inc., *Toronto*
Prentice-Hall Hispanoamericana, S.A., *Mexico*
Prentice-Hall of India Private Limited, *New Delhi*
Prentice-Hall of Japan, Inc., *Tokyo*
Prentice-Hall (Singapore) Pte. Ltd., *Singapore*
Editora Prentice-Hall do Brasil, Ltda., *Rio de Janeiro*

# Contents

*Introduction*   xi

*Acknowledgments*   xiii

*About the Author*   xiv

**Chapter 1**   The Basics   1

Introduction   2
  Drawing Toolbar   2
  Movie Properties   4
  Work Area and Zoom   5
  Drawing Simple Shapes and Text   6
  Undo Levels   7
  Selecting Graphics   8

Drawing and Modifying Text   9
  Creating the Text Layer   10
  Setting Text Properties   11
  Creating Title Text   12
  Creating Shadow Text   14
  Linking Text   16
  Moving Text   19

Drawing and Modifying Shapes   20
  Creating Circles   21

Duplicating the Circle and Moving the
    Duplicates  22
Connecting Circles with Lines  25
Creating the Background Curve  27
Creating the Background Fill  29
Texture Fills and Transparency  34
    Creating New Fill for Circles  34
    Changing Fill of Circles  34
    Creating and Modifying the Transparent Circle  36
Importing Graphics  38
    Importing an Image  38
    Changing the Photo Settings  38

**Chapter 2**    Animating the Page  41
Timelines and Frames  41
    Creating the Link Text Symbol  42
    Creating the Logo Layer  42
    Adding an Additional Background Layer  44
    Creating Some Layers for the Circles  44
    Frames and Animation  45
    Tweening and Keyframes  46
    Adding Keyframes to the Shelley Biotech Page  47
Movement Tweening  48
    Animating the Tan Background Curve  48
    A Quick Word about Onion-Skinning  51
    Animating the Link Spheres  51
    Animating the Address Text  55
    Animating the Text Links  57
    Animating the Header Text  58
Shape Tweening  59
    Creating the Beginning S Shape  59
    Applying Shape Tweening to the S  61
    Adding Shape Hints  62
Fading  64
    Fading in the White Background  64
    Fading in the Office Photo  65
    Fading in the Logo Lines  66
    Changing the Color of the Text Links  67
    Fading in the Link Spheres  68
    Changing the Color of the Address Text  69

**Chapter 3**    Making the Page Interactive    71

Symbols    71
  Creating Symbols    72
  Using the Library to Access Your Symbols    72
  Editing Symbols    72
  Changing Symbol Types    74

Creating Buttons    74
  Changing the Link Circle Symbol's Properties    75
  Changing the Instance Properties for the Link
    Spheres    75
  Adding the Web Links to the Buttons    77
  Testing the Links    78

Button Actions    79
  Opening the Button Frame Action Window    79
  Adding the Keyframes for Button Actions    80
  Creating the Hit Frame    81
  Creating the Over Frame    82
  Creating the Down Frame    83
  Testing the Button Actions    85

Sound Effects    86
  Adding a Sound to the Library    86
  Using the Macromedia Sound Library    86
  Adding Sound to the Buttons    87
  Testing the Sound Effect    88

**Chapter 4**    Publishing to the Web    91

Finishing Touches    91
  Deciding What Resolution to Use    92
  Deciding Which Platforms to Use    93
  Deciding Which Flash Version or File Type to Use    94

Publishing    94
  Choosing Format Settings    94
  Choosing Flash Settings    96
  Choosing HTML Settings    97
  Publishing the Movie    99
  Viewing the Size Report    99
  Optimizing the Movie    101
  Writing the HTML for the .swf File    102
  Creating a Non-Flash Version of the Page    103
  A Few Final Web Publishing Issues    106

Preloading  107
Adding a Scene to the Current Movie  107
Modifying the Preload Scene  108
Creating the Preloading Animation  109
Adding the Action Code  111
Putting in a Stop Action  113
Detecting the Plug-In  114
Modifying the Movie for Flash Detection  115
Creating the HTML Page for This Movie  117
Web Server Settings  118
Configuring Apache  118
Configuring IIS 4.0  118

Chapter 5  Fine-Tuning Graphics  121
Reshaping  121
Getting Started  122
Drawing the Needle Graphic  123
Filling in Needle Texture  126
Tilting the Needle  127
Drawing the Thread  128
Intersections  129
Creating the Button Texture  130
Creating the Buttonholes  132
Adding the Thread Fill to the Buttonholes  134
Creating the Text  135
Coloring the Text  138
Adding the Photographic Image  139
Brush Effects  140
Creating the Shadow for the Button and Photo  140
Creating Gradient for Shadows  142
Modifying the Shadow Gradient  143

Chapter 6  Advanced Animation  147
Animating Symbols  147
Creating the Button Symbol  148
Animating the Button  149
Creating Other Symbols  152
Opening Sequence  152
Getting Started  153
Moving the Button Image  153

Fading in the Thread Image 156
Stitch Text Animation and Fading 157
Fashion Text Animation and Fading 161
Blues Text with Motion Layer 165
Needle Rotation, Fading, and Movement 168
Text Shadow Movement, Shape, and Tint 169
Photograph Fade-in 171
Background Music 172
Creating the New Movie 172
Creating the First Button 173
Creating the Second Button 174
Creating the Movie Clip 175
Inserting the Buttons in the Movie 176
Modifying the Action Layer 176
Adding the Music Layer 179
Adding the Clip to the Movie 180
Adding the Clip to the Splash Screen 185

**Chapter 7**   Advanced Effects 187
Animated Buttons 187
Creating the Parent Button 188
Creating the Movie Clip 189
Adding the Movie Clip to the Button Over State 190
Transitions 191
Creating a New Scene 191
Copying Frames 192
Fading Out Images 194
Moving and Resizing the Other Images 195
Adding More Motion to the Button Symbol 198
Putting in the Link Buttons 198
Adding the Articles and Photos 202
Lengthening the Thread 204
Stopping the Action at the End of the Menu Scene
Animation 204
Forms 205
Creating the Form 206
Setting the Variables 209
Creating a New Scene 210
Adding the Actions 210
Interactive Activity 212
Getting Started 212

Adding the Static Elements   213
Creating a Movie Clip   215
Adding the Colored Buttons   216
Adding Some Text Labels   218
Applying the Action to the First Button   219
Applying the Action to the Second Button   221
Applying Actions to the Third and Fourth
    Buttons   222
Setting Actions for the First Keyframe   222
Creating the Movie Clip for the Second
    Keyframe   223
Applying the Action to the First Button   224
Setting Actions for the Second Keyframe   226
Adding Next and Previous Buttons   227
Final Production: Publishing   230

**Appendix A**   Flash 4 Reference   231

*Index*   251

# Introduction

*The first time I tried to create graphics with Flash, I loved it. After one week of experimenting with the program, I was convinced that it was one of the best Web development applications on the market. However, I was a bit disappointed by the lack of resources available for learning how to use it. The tutorials from Macromedia were useful, but they lacked depth. It was then that I realized that a hands-on, step-by-step book describing how to create Flash Web sites would be extremely useful to Web professionals who wanted to learn the essentials of Flash quickly and easily.*

Welcome to *Essential Flash 4 for Web Professionals*! In these pages, you'll learn how to create wonderful Flash animations and interactive activities including:

- Quick-loading vector graphics
- Impressive animations
- Shape morphing
- Buttons with actions and Web links
- Buttons and movies with sound and music
- Interactive movies
- Simple Web forms

In addition, we'll discuss how to optimize Flash movies for better download, detect the plug-in, and pre-load Flash.

# ◆ How to Use This Book

This book consists of step-by-step instructions for creating two hypothetical Web sites. First, we'll create a straight-forward Flash site for Shelley Biotech, with simple vector graphics created in Flash, basic animation, animated buttons, and buttons with sound. Then, we'll design a Web site for *Stitch Fashion Journal* that includes a splash screen with music and a music on/off control. You'll also learn how to create more advanced graphics and animation, an interactive dressing room, and an e-mail form.

All you need to do is follow the instructions to create the sites. As you work through the steps, you'll be presented with checkpoints where you should save your work. In addition, these checkpoints will provide a URL to the book's Web site, from which you can download the project at various stages of completion. That way, if you have difficulty with portions of the project, you can access the files and learn how to accomplish specific steps. The Web site for this book is located at http://www.phptr.com/essential/flash.

If you have any difficulty with the instructions presented in this book, or if you would just like to drop me a line about it, you can reach me by e-mail at lynn@rainc.com.

# Acknowledgments

Many thanks to M.J. Wilson of MJ Wilson Photography (http://www.beautybytes.com/photomj) for the wonderful photographs and to Cheryl Boyle and Nicole Daulton for posing for them. Chrissy Rey (http://www.flashlite.net) provided me with very helpful advice for creating the music toggle. Thanks to Gus Mueller (http://www.gusmueller.com) for the sound files used in the *Stitch* site.

Thanks to Rachel Collett for the many excellent suggestions and to Cary Collett for the introduction. Thanks to Paul Saab for giving me a place to host my sites and test my work. I'm also grateful to Karen McLean and Dan Livingston for giving me this opportunity and being so patient. But most importantly, Michael, thanks for your extensive help and patience. I finally finished it!

# About the Author

Lynn Kyle has been a Web professional since 1992. She has worked for the Naval Research Laboratory as a computer scientist and more recently was a Webmaster at Los Alamos National Laboratory. Currently, she is the owner of her own Web design firm, Ricochet Associates. Lynn has received many honors for her Web design, including mention in *PC Magazine's* Top 100 Web Sites and Point Com's Top 5% of the Web, as well as print recognition in major publications such as the *New York Times*, *Newsweek*, and the *Los Angeles Times*. Some of her clients include Lloyd's of London, Pfizer, and DeBeers.

# 1 The Basics

## IN THIS CHAPTER

- Introduction
- Drawing and Modifying Text
- Drawing and Modifying Shapes
- Texture Fills and Transparency
- Importing Graphics
- Recap
- Advanced Projects

*It's 4:59 P.M. on Friday afternoon. You have just found the perfect spot to prop up your feet in your cubicle. Suddenly your boss pokes his head in. Your heart starts to pound.*

*"Just got out of a meeting with Mr. Big," your boss says. "He heard that all the best Web sites are now using Flash, and he wants us to use it as well. So what exactly is Flash?"*

*"It's uh . . . er . . . a really exciting new Web technology," you guess.*

*"Oh good, you know all about it. Here's the Flash 4 software. Mr. Big wants us to take our current homepage and turn it into a Flash site by Monday. Is that going to be a problem?"*

*Being the ambitious, ready-to-go-home-for-the-weekend kind of person you are, you decide your best bet is to tell him what he wants to hear.*

*"Monday. No problem."*

*"I'm counting on you. Have a nice weekend!" Your boss departs, leaving you slightly lightheaded.*

*Okay. Don't panic. You can re-create your company's homepage in Flash and still have time to go rock climbing this weekend. Open that Flash 4 box! Let's begin with the basics.*

# ◆ Introduction

We will start with a quick and painless overview of some of Flash's features. If you'd rather get right to creating the exciting new Shelley Biotech homepage, jump on down to "Drawing and Modifying Text."

At this point Flash should be installed on your machine. If it is not, please install it.

What's so special about Flash animation? Flash is an application that allows you to create quick-loading vector-based animations, interactive activities, and forms for the Web. A vector image file consists of a list of points to be connected. Graphics used on the Web, such as JPEGs and GIFs, are known as *raster* graphics. Raster graphic files are much larger than vector-type files because they describe the entire image, using an x-y coordinate system. Vector graphics are much smaller because their files consist of mathematical descriptions of the graphics. Instead of each pixel of an image having to be described, a vector-based image is described in terms of connecting lines and points. In addition to being smaller files, vector images can be resized without a loss of detail.

The Flash interface. Start the Flash program. When you first begin, you will be presented with a new, blank movie as shown in Figure 1–1.

Each movie can contain multiple *scenes*. A scene consists of a timeline, layers, and a work area where you create the graphics. The timeline is used for adding animation. Each scene can have multiple layers, useful for animating images separately.

## Drawing Toolbar

The Drawing toolbar is shown in Figure 1–2. These are the basic tools used to create and modify vector graphics in Flash. As we take

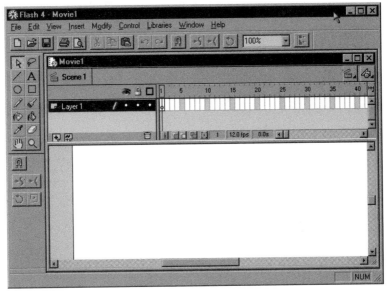

**FIGURE 1-1** The Flash interface

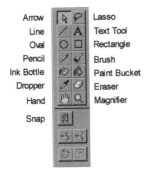

**FIGURE 1-2** The Drawing toolbar

a brief look at each tool, select it and notice that the options underneath the toolbar change. If you hold your mouse cursor over an item on the interface for a few seconds, its name will appear.

- The Arrow tool is used to select graphic objects you have created.
- The Lasso tool is also for selecting, but it allows you to select part of a graphic object.
- Three basic shape-drawing tools are on the toolbar: the Line, Oval, and Rectangle. If you click on each of these, you

should notice that the options for the particular tool are presented at the bottom of the toolbar. This is where you can change the color, line thickness, and line style. The Oval and Rectangle also have some fill option settings.
- The Pencil allows you to draw curved lines.
- The Brush tool is for creating free-form shapes.
- If you create a shape and you want to change the line style or fill, you can edit these with the Ink Bottle and Paint Bucket.
- The Dropper is used to identify the fill color or line style in use on a particular graphic.
- The Eraser can be used to erase portions of a particular graphic.
- The Magnifier and the Hand are used to change the view of the scene rather than to manipulate graphics. The Magnifier lets you zoom in or out, and the Hand can be used to move the entire scene around.

## Movie Properties

As you create a Flash movie, you will need to modify some of the default settings for the movie, such as size and background color. These and other movie characteristics can be changed using the Movie Properties dialog box, shown in Figure 1–3. To open this dialog box, choose Modify→Movie.

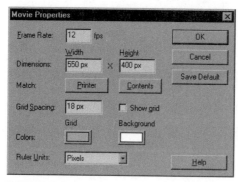

**FIGURE 1–3** Movie Properties dialog box

- The Frame Rate determines how many frames per second (fps) will be shown. A higher fps means your movie will play faster and be shorter than a low fps, as well as seeming smoother.

- The Dimensions are displayed in pixels. Keep in mind that Flash allows you the choice of either hardwiring the height and width or allowing the movie to scale to fit the browser window.

- Flash provides you with a grid you can use to help in moving graphics around. Grid Spacing specifies the distance between lines of the grid.

- This dialog box also lets you change the color of the grid and the background. If you decided on a gray background, you would want to change the grid color to something else to make it more visible.

- Finally, the Units drop box lets you change the size units used for your movie to something other than pixels.

## *Work Area and Zoom*

The grid is a tool that helps you adjust your graphics. To demonstrate the Work Area and Zoom features, turn the grid on by choosing View→Grid. The grid should now be visible on your movie.

Use the Magnifier tool with the plus and minus options to enlarge and shrink the movie view. You can also use the Zoom list box on the top menu to change the view size. See the Zoom list box on the right side of Figure 1–4.

**FIGURE 1–4** The top toolbar with the Zoom list box

The dimensions of the movie are set in the Movie Properties dialog box. There will be times when you want to create a graphic larger than the movie height and width, or animate a graphic moving onto the movie from outside of the scene. The Work Area option under View is useful for seeing graphics that are off the scene. This may be useful when you want a graphic to move on or off the scene or to be much larger than the scene itself. Figure 1–5 shows the same movie with the Work Area option turned off on the left and turned on on the right.

**FIGURE 1–5** Work Area option shown turned off and on

## Drawing Simple Shapes and Text

Several basic shapes are shown on the toolbar: the Line, Oval, and Rectangle. The Line tool allows you to draw straight lines of varying widths, colors, and styles. Figure 1–6 shows some of the lines you can draw by selecting various attributes.

**FIGURE 1–6** Line styles

The Oval tool allows you to draw various oval shapes. They can be filled or unfilled, with or without a border. See Figure 1–7 for some examples.

**FIGURE 1–7** Assorted ovals

To draw a rectangle, use the Rectangle tool. The options for this tool are the same as for the Oval. The Round Rectangle

Radius button lets you create rectangles with curved corners (see Figure 1–8).

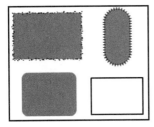

**FIGURE 1–8** Assorted rectangles

You can create text with the Text tool, which allows you to create text with various font styles, sizes, and colors. Figure 1–9 shows some text with various fonts and sizes. Notice in the figure that the text is antialiased. To view the antialiased text, choose View→Antialias Text. You will probably want to do this each time you start creating a new movie. The last text example shows two different fonts in the same text string. You can change the font, color, or size at any time while you are creating text.

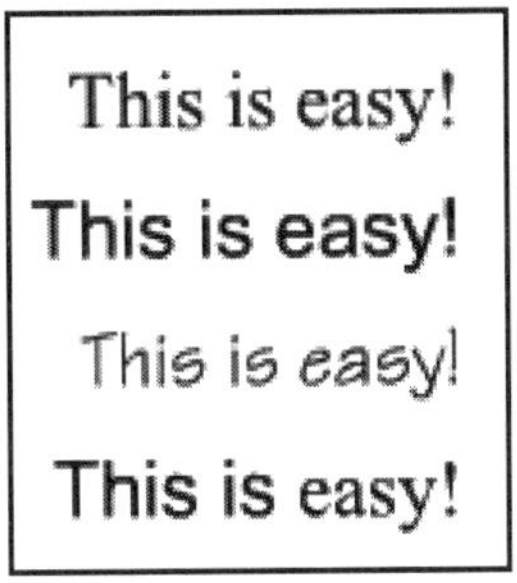

This is easy!

This is easy!

This is easy!

This is easy!

**FIGURE 1–9** Assorted text fonts

## Undo Levels

One of the best features of Flash is the Undo Levels setting under File→Preferences. The number of Undo Levels indicated on the File Preferences specifies how many times you can choose the Undo option. As you might guess, selecting Edit→Undo undoes the last thing you did. Obviously it's great if you have made a mistake, or if you just want to try out several things from the same starting point. Figure 1–10 shows the File Preferences dialog box with the Undo Levels set to 100. A word of caution: The multi-frame nature of animations in Flash may cause you some confusion. For example, if you draw a line in one frame, change to a different frame, and choose Edit→Undo, it will delete the line, but you won't be able to tell that it has done so unless you click on the original frame in which you drew the line.

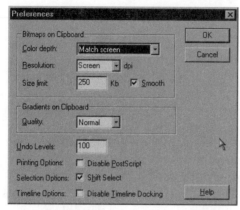

**FIGURE 1–10** File Preferences dialog box

## *Selecting Graphics*

It is most important to know how to select and deselect graphics in Flash. To select a single graphic object, click on it with the Arrow from the toolbar. To deselect an object, click on it a second time. When a graphic is selected, its appearance will change, as shown in Figure 1–11. The first circle and its outline are not selected. The second one shows just the fill selected. The third one has the outline selected, and the fourth shows both the fill and the outline selected. To select multiple objects, hold down the Shift key while clicking with the Arrow.

Enough with the preliminaries; let's start creating that page!

**FIGURE 1–11** Unselected and selected circle fills and borders

# ◆ Drawing and Modifying Text

Figure 1–12 shows the current Shelley Biotech homepage. Because the boss likes the current page, we first have to re-create it with Flash. To view the current unflashed page on the Web, go to http://www.phptr.com/essential/flash/shelley/old/. If you'd like to see where we're going, look at the finished Flash version at http://www.phptr.com/essential/flash/shelley/new/.

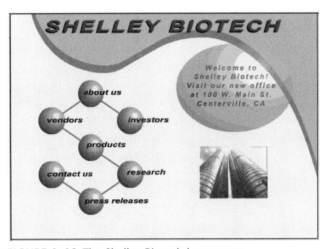

**FIGURE 1–12** The Shelley Biotech homepage

To begin creating a Flash version of this page:

1.  Select the menu option File→New. A new blank movie opens. Next, choose File→Save As. Save this file in the directory of your choice as shelley.fla.

2.  Select the menu option Modify→Movie. Change the dimensions of your movie to 700 pixels in width and 500 pixels in height. Change the Grid Spacing in this same dialog box to 20 pixels (see Figure 1–13). Select OK.

Since we are going to re-create the Shelley Biotech homepage, we will examine each element on the page separately. You can see that we will need to create text. Creating graphic text can be done with most graphics programs, but the advantage to creating it in Flash is that we can later animate it. Let's start by creating a layer.

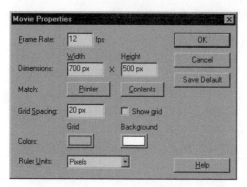

**FIGURE 1–13** Movie Properties dialog box

## Creating the Text Layer

Because we are going to work with so many different objects that we will want to animate separately, we should put each object type in a distinct layer.

1. To create a new layer, click on the Add Layer icon below the Layer 1 label, as in Figure 1–14. You can also use the menu option Insert→Layer.

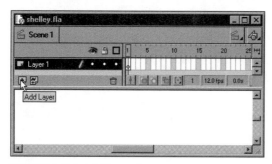

**FIGURE 1–14** Add Layer icon

2. Now Layer 2 appears above Layer 1. To give Layer 2 a more meaningful name, double-click on its name so that it is highlighted, and type in the words "Header Text;" then press Enter.

3. Finally, click on the Header Text layer to make sure it is the currently selected one. The currently selected layer will have a pencil icon to its right, and its name will appear as white text on a black background.

## Setting Text Properties

We need to set the properties for our header.

1. Begin by selecting the Text tool. You will now change the settings for this text in the next few steps. To make sure you are on the right track, see Figure 1–15 as you complete these steps.

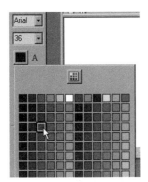

**FIGURE 1–15** Color palette

2. Select the Arial font from the first drop-down list below the tools. If you do not have this font, substitute another one for all text mentioned in this example.

3. Select a font size of 36 from the second drop-down list.

4. Click on the Text Color button. This is the button with a black square on it under the Font Size list box. A palette box will open. Choose the color in the third column and fourth row. Another way to choose the color is to click on the button at the top of the palette box. A dialog box will appear. You can specify the color by RGB values, in this case (0, 102, 102), as shown in Figure 1–16.

5. After setting the RGB values in this dialog box, close it by clicking on the X icon on the top right corner. This dialog box is a bit confusing because it does not have a Close button. The Change button is used to change one of the preset palette colors to something else, so for now it's best just to close the dialog box with the X.

6. Finally, click on both the Bold and Italic buttons under the Text preferences, as in Figure 1–17.

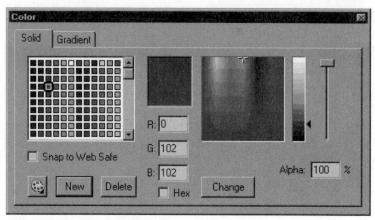

**FIGURE 1–16** Palette dialog box

**FIGURE 1–17** Font properties

## Creating Title Text

We will now create the title text.

1.  Select the menu options View→Grid and View→Snap. Snap can be also be turned on and off using the Snap button located on the top toolbar, and as an option when the Arrow tool is used. The Snap option causes graphics to align themselves with the grid automatically.

2.  With the Text tool selected, click somewhere near the upper-left corner of the Scene and type "SHELLEY BIOTECH."

3.  Change to the Arrow tool. The text you created should be surrounded by a selection box (see Figure 1–18). If it is

not, try clicking on the header text with the Arrow until you see a box around it.

**FIGURE 1–18** Header with selection box

4. Click somewhere else on the work area to deselect the text.

5. The text may look a little jagged. To view the text with antialiasing, select the menu item View→Antialias Text. The text you just created should no longer appear jagged.

6. The text needs to be stretched out. Earlier we set the grid to 20 pixels x 20 pixels. With the Arrow tool selected, click on the Scale button, as shown in Figure 1–19. This button is located on the bottom right of the toolbar.

**FIGURE 1–19** Scale button

7. You will now see handles on the selection box (see Figure 1–20).

**FIGURE 1–20** Selection box with handles

8. Select the menu option Window→Inspectors→Object. This shows us the X, Y locations and the height and width of the currently selected object.

9. Our text is not wide enough. We want it to be approximately 600 pixels, or 30 grid lines in length. There are two ways to do this: The first way is to click and hold the right-hand center handle and drag to the right to make the text wider. The second is to change the width value to 600 and click Apply in the Object Inspector dialog box, as shown in Figure 1–21.

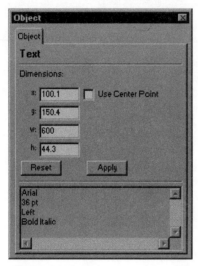

**FIGURE 1–21**  Object Inspector dialog box

**NOTE**

This would be a good time to save your work. Choose File→Save As, and save this file as shelley.fla in the directory of your choice. Download the project at this point from http://www.phptr.com/essential/flash/shelley/shelley1-1.html.

## Creating Shadow Text

Looking at the static Shelley page at http://www.phptr.com/essential/flash/shelley/old/ and Figure 1–22, you will notice that the header text appears to have a shadow under it. Let's create this effect.

# *SHELLEY BIOTECH*

**FIGURE 1–22** Header with shadow

1.  With the header text selected, click on the Scale button to turn off that option. The handles should disappear, but the header should have a selection box around it.

2.  Select the menu option Edit→Copy.

3.  Now select Edit→Paste. A new copy of the header text appears.

4.  Use the Arrow to select the original header. Notice that you can select more than one object at a time by holding down the Shift key and selecting with the Arrow at the same time. If you have a selection box around both copies, click somewhere else on the screen to deselect both. You can also right-click on a PC or Ctrl-click on a Mac to bring up a menu with a Deselect All option.

5.  With just the original header selected, select the Text tool.

6.  Change the color of the current header to black by clicking on the Text Color button on the toolbar and selecting black from the palette.

7.  Change to the Arrow tool. Select both header texts using the Arrow and the Shift key.

8.  Click on the Align button on the menu bar. It's located on the right of the Zoom Control drop-down box as shown in Figure 1–23.

**FIGURE 1–23** Top toolbar with the Align button

9.  Since the two headers are exactly the same size, you can use any of the align options. Select one of the three vertical align options, and one of the three horizontal align options (see Figure 1–24). Then click OK.

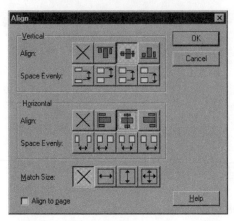

**FIGURE 1–24** Align dialog box

**10.** Both headers are selected, with one on top of the other. Deselect both, then click on the green header, which should be the only one visible. Using the Arrow keys to move it one pixel at a time, move it to the right 3 pixels and up 2 pixels.

**11.** With the Arrow, click and hold on a blank area of the scene to the left and above the headers, and drag to the right and below them. Release the mouse button. At this point, both headers are selected again.

**12.** Since we now have the two headers aligned appropriately, we should group them together. Choose the menu option Modify→Group. The two headers will now behave like a single object. They can be ungrouped at any time with the Modify→Ungroup command.

**NOTE**
This would be a good time to save your work or download the project at this point from http://www.phptr.com/essential/flash/shelley/ shelley1-2.html.

## Linking Text

We need to create the text that will be used for page links, shown in Figure 1–25.

**FIGURE 1–25** Link text

1. A new layer for our links would be a good idea. Click on the Add Layer button. Layer 3 now appears. Double-click on Layer 3 to rename it "Link Text." We should use Layer 1 for something, so rename it "Address Text."

2. Select the Link Text layer and right-click (PC) or Ctrl-click (Mac) to access the Layer menu. From the Layer menu, select Hide Others. The Header layer will no longer be visible.

3. Select the Text tool. The font should be Arial, font size 16, font color black, and both Bold and Italic should be selected (see Figure 1–26).

**FIGURE 1–26** The Text setting for the Links and the Address Text

4. Type the first link, *about us*. Click away from the text once to finish. Then click elsewhere on the scene and type the next link, *vendors*.

5. Repeat until all the links have been typed as separate objects. The links are *about us, vendors, investors, products, contact us, research,* and *press releases.*

Now, let's add the address text to the scene.

1. Click on the Address Text layer to select it and right-click (PC) or Ctrl-click (Mac) to open the Layer menu. Select Hide Others from the Layer menu.

2. Select the Text tool and change the text color to the green color you used for the header. The font is Arial, the size is 16, and it is both bold and italicized, just like the links.

3. Change the text alignment by selecting the Center option from the Alignment button on the bottom left of the toolbar, as shown in Figure 1–27.

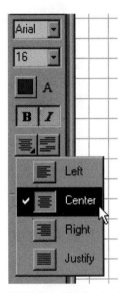

**FIGURE 1–27** Center button

4. Click on the scene and type "Welcome to Shelley Biotech! Visit our new office at 100 W. Main St. Centerville, CA." Use the Enter key to type new lines, as shown in Figure 1–28.

5. Select the Arrow tool. The Address text should look like Figure 1–28.

All the text for the page has been created!

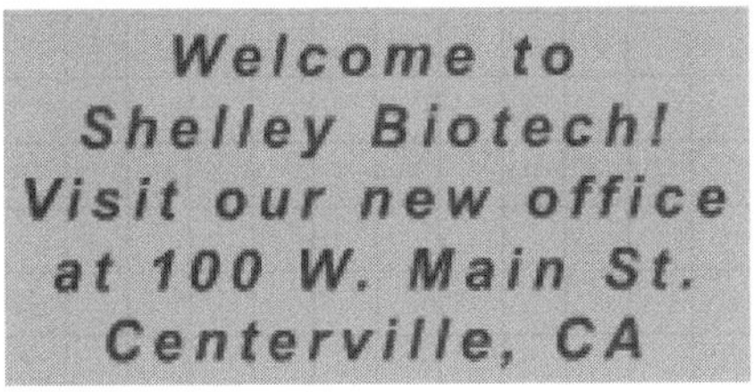

> *Welcome to*
> *Shelley Biotech!*
> *Visit our new office*
> *at 100 W. Main St.*
> *Centerville, CA*

**FIGURE 1–28** Address text

**NOTE**
This would be a good time to save your work or download the project at this point from http://www.phptr.com/essential/flash/shelley/shelley1-3.html.

## Moving Text

As the last step, we will place the text objects in the appropriate locations on the page.

1. Choose the menu option View→Rulers.

2. Turn off Snap by either unchecking the menu option View→Snap or deselecting the Snap icon on the toolbar.

3. Click on the Header Text layer and hide the other layers using the Layer menu. The Layer menu can be opened by right-clicking (PC) or Ctrl-clicking (Mac) on the Header Text layer.

4. Open the Object Inspector dialog box by selecting the menu option Window→Inspectors→Object.

5. Change the values in the Object Inspector dialog box to an X location of 70 and a Y location of 5. Click Apply. (See Figure 1–29.)

6. Click on the Address Text layer and hide the other layers with the Layer menu.

7. Move it to approximately X of 16 and Y of 335 with the Object Inspector dialog box. Press the Apply button.

8. Click on the Link Text layer and hide the others.

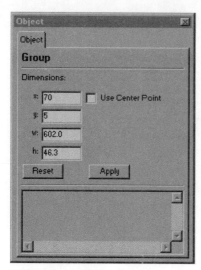

**FIGURE 1–29** Object Inspector dialog box

9. For now, use the Arrow to move all the link headers, one at a time, to the lower-right corner of the scene. Don't worry about exact locations; we just want to get them out of the way.

10. Close the Object Inspector by clicking on the X in the upper right of the dialog box.

**NOTE**
This would be a good time to save your work or download the project at this point from http://www.phptr.com/essential/flash/shelley/shelley1-4.html.

## ◆ Drawing and Modifying Shapes

We now need to create some of the shapes for this page. We will start with the filled circles, then move on to lines, and finally to curves. You should be using a screen resolution of at least 800 pixels x 600 pixels. As we progress through this section we will be creating many layers. You can make it easier to see the layers by clicking and dragging on the bar between the layer list and the work area, as shown in Figure 1–30. Notice how the cursor changes when it is moved over the dividing bar.

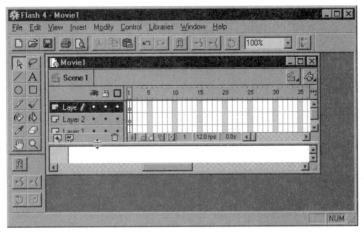

**FIGURE 1–30** Dragging the layer list down to make it larger

## Creating Circles

1. Create a new layer and call it "Circles." Hide the other layers.

2. If the grid is not showing, select the menu options View→ Grid. Make sure Snap is active by selecting View→Snap.

3. Select the Oval tool. You will need to set the line color to transparent. To do this, click on the Line Color palette button and select the blank square in the upper-left corner of the palette (see Figure 1–31).

**FIGURE 1–31** Setting the line color to transparent

4. Change the other settings below the Tool palette to match the ones in Figure 1–32. Choose any gray from the Fill Color. Select 1.0 for the line thickness, and Solid for the line style.

**FIGURE 1–32** Line settings

5. Click and hold the mouse button in the scene to draw a circle. Make the circle 60 pixels x 60 pixels, or 3 grid lines x 3 grid lines as in Figure 1–33. Remember that the grid is set to 20 pixels. Release the mouse button.

**FIGURE 1–33** Circle

The flat gray circle is rather boring, so we will be changing the fill shortly.

**NOTE**

This would be a good time to save your work or download the project at this point from http://www.phptr.com/essential/flash/shelley/ shelley1-5.html.

## Duplicating the Circle and Moving the Duplicates

You have a single gray circle, but you'll need seven of them to create the logo image seen in Figure 1–34. We will start by duplicating them.

**FIGURE 1–34** Links with circles

1. You could simply copy and paste the circles, but since we are going to change the fill later, it's much easier to make a symbol. Select the gray circle with the Arrow tool. The advantage to making this graphic a symbol is that it allows us to easily add more instances to the work area without having to redraw the circle each time. Also, only symbols can have actions associated with them, which will be important when we turn this into a button later.

2. Choose the menu item Insert→Convert to Symbol. In the Symbol Properties dialog box shown in Figure 1–35, call it "Link Circle" and leave its Behavior set to Graphic. Click OK.

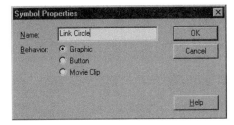

**FIGURE 1–35** Symbol Properties dialog box

3. To duplicate the circle, select Window→Library. This displays all the symbols that have been created (see Figure 1–36).

4. We have created only one symbol, the Link Circle, so far. Click and hold on the Link Circle in the Library window

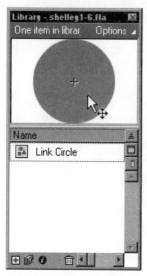

**FIGURE 1–36** Duplicating the circle

and drag it to the scene. Do this five more times until you have seven circles on the scene.

5. Turn off Snap.

6. Open the Object Inspector dialog box.

7. Move all the circles to the upper-right corner of the work area, out of the way.

8. Move the circles to the following (X,Y) locations: (135, 138), (220, 80), (305, 138), (220, 196), (135, 254), (220, 312), and (305, 254). Whew!

The circles should now be in the configuration shown in Figure 1–37.

**NOTE**

This would be a good time to save your work or download the project at this point from http://www.phptr.com/essential/flash/shelley/shelley1-6.html.

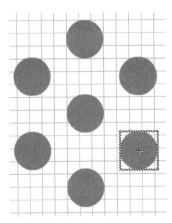

**FIGURE 1–37** Circle configuration

## Connecting Circles with Lines

As you can see from Figure 1–37, we need to draw some lines connecting the circles.

1. Select the Line tool. Change the Line Thickness to 4.0, and the Line Style to Solid (see Figure 1–38).

**FIGURE 1–38** Line settings

2. Open the Color palette by clicking on the Line Color button. Click on the button at the top of the palette as shown in Figure 1–39. This will open the Color dialog box.

3. Change the color to RGB of 153, 153, 102 (see Figure 1–40). Click on New to add this color to the palette. Notice that the palette has a scroll bar next to it. To see the color you just added, you may need to scroll. Click on the upper-right corner of the dialog box to close it.

**FIGURE 1–39** Color palette

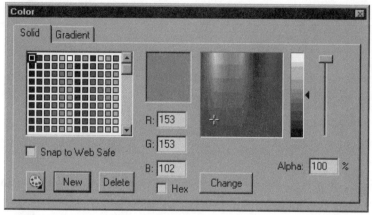

**FIGURE 1–40** Color dialog box

   **4.** Turn on Snap.

   **5.** Press and hold down the mouse button at the center of the top circle. While still holding, move the mouse to the center of the circle to the right and below. Release. You should now have a line connecting two of the circles (see Figure 1–41).

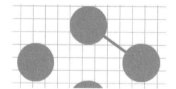

**FIGURE 1–41** First connecting line

   **6.** Continue drawing lines to make an S shape, as in Figure 1–42.

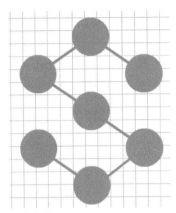

**FIGURE 1–42** Circles with all the connecting lines

7. Select all the line segments and the circles by dragging a large rectangle around everything with the Arrow tool. Choose Modify→Group.

**NOTE**

This would be a good time to save your work or download the project at this point from http://www.phptr.com/essential/flash/shelley/shelley1-7.html.

## Creating the Background Curve

The background will be created from a rectangle with one side curved (see Figure 1–11).

1. To make our animation a bit more interesting, we will make the true background color a light tan. Select the menu item Modify→Movie. In the Movie Properties dialog box, change the Background color to the fifth column, third row from the bottom. It's a light tan color. Click OK.

2. Time to create yet another layer. In addition to choosing Insert→Layer, you can also create layers with the Layer menu by choosing Insert Layer. Name this new layer "Background." Select Hide Others from the Layer menu.

3. If all those layers are crowding the scene window, move your mouse to the border between the scene and the frame around it until the cursor changes as shown in Figure 1–30. Click and drag upward.

4. The easiest way to draw a curve is to create a line and then modify it. Change to the Line tool. Select black for the color, H for the line thickness, and Solid for the line style. H stands for *hairline*.

5. With Snap and Grid on, draw two line segments as shown in Figure 1–43. For the first segment, click and hold and move the mouse to the right 3 grid lines and down 4 grid lines. Start the second at the end of the first and move to the right 6 grid lines and down 7 grid lines.

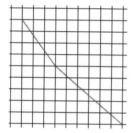

**FIGURE 1–43** Two line segments

6. Let's turn those lines into curves. Change to the Arrow tool. Move the cursor over the first line segment. When it changes to an arrow with a curve under it, click and hold and pull the line downward until it resembles Figure 1–44. Don't forget about Edit→Undo!

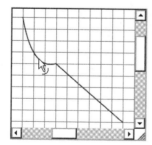

**FIGURE 1–44** First line segment curved

**7.** Curve the second line segment, as shown in Figure 1–45.

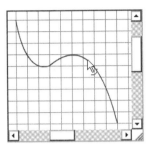

**FIGURE 1–45** Second line segment curved

**NOTE**

This would be a good time to save your work or download the project at this point from http://www.phptr.com/essential/flash/shelley/ shelley1-8.html.

## Creating the Background Fill

You now have the curve that will be used to form the background. We will make it a solid filled object and then duplicate it.

**1.** Change to the Rectangle tool. Select black for the line color, H for the line thickness, and Solid for the line style.

**2.** The rectangle should not have a fill color. To set the fill color to transparent, click on the Fill Color button and click on the empty square at the top left of the palette (see Figure 1–46).

**FIGURE 1–46** Setting the rectangle fill color to transparent

3. Draw a rectangle beginning with the top left of the curve and ending at the bottom right. You should now have a curve surrounded by a rectangle.

4. Change to the Arrow tool, hold down the Shift key, and click on the top and the right side of the rectangle to select both. Select the menu item Edit→Clear, or the Delete key on your keyboard. You should now have a shape that looks like Figure 1–47.

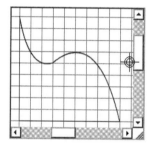

**FIGURE 1–47** Second line segment curved

5. Change to the Paint Bucket. Click on the Fill Color button.

6. Click on the button at the top of the palette to open the Color dialog box.

7. On the Solid tab, set the color to RGB of 153, 153, 102 (see Figure 1–48). Close this dialog box.

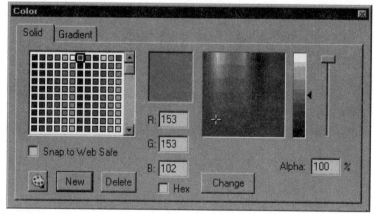

**FIGURE 1–48** Color dialog box

8. Click inside the figure to color it.

9. Delete the border by changing to the Arrow, holding down the Shift key, selecting the outline of the curve and the left and bottom edges, and pressing the Delete key.

10. Select the object.

11. Select Edit→Copy and Edit→Paste. Click and drag this copy until no part of it is on top of the original.

12. Change the color of the new object we just created. Change its color to white by clicking the Paint Bucket, setting the color to white, and clicking on the new shape.

13. Turn these shapes into symbols by selecting each with the Arrow and choosing Insert→Convert to Symbol. Name one "White Background" and one "Brown Background," leave them as graphics, and press OK. You should have two curve shapes, as shown in Figure 1–49.

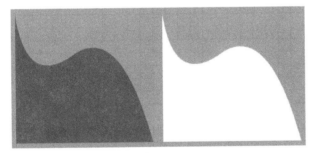

**FIGURE 1–49** Two curve shapes

14. Select both of them and choose Modify→Align on the standard toolbar. Choose vertical align center and horizontal align center (see the Align dialog box in Figure 1–50.) Click OK.

15. You should now only see the white shape. If you see the brown shape you need to change the order. Deselect both and then click on the brown shape. Choose Modify→Arrange→Send to Back.

16. We need to make these shapes much larger. Change to the Magnifier tool and choose the Reduce option. Click in the scene to reduce it to about 50%. You can tell what the current magnification is by looking at the Zoom list box on the top toolbar. Choose the menu option View→Work Area.

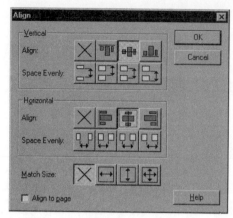

**FIGURE 1–50** Align dialog box

**17.** Change to the Arrow tool. Choose Edit→Select All. Click and drag the shapes to the upper-left corner of the screen.

**18.** Click on the Scale button at the bottom right of the left toolbar. Move the shapes and pull and drag the handles to make it resemble Figure 1–51.

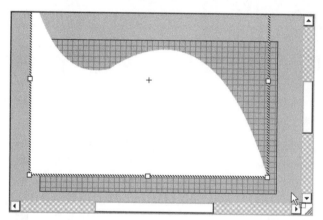

**FIGURE 1–51** Moving and resizing the white background shape

**19.** Deselect the images. Click on the top one with the Arrow and move it downward so it is offset from the brown about 20 pixels (see Figure 1–52).

**20.** Turn off the workspace view by unchecking Edit→View Work Area.

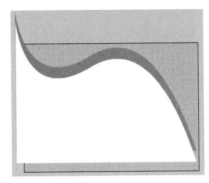

**FIGURE 1–52** Alignment of background shapes

**21.** Right-click (PC) or Ctrl-click (Mac) on the layer list to pull up the Layer menu. Choose Show All from the Layer menu. The background layer needs to be moved to the back. To do this, click and hold on the layer name and pull downward until you reach the bottom of the list.

**22.** Now that you have all the layers visible, move the graphics to roughly where they belong. You will need to move the Link Text layer above the Circles layer.

Figure 1–53 shows the current project with all the layers visible.

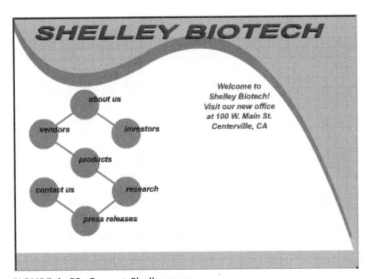

**FIGURE 1–53** Current Shelley page

**NOTE**

This would be a good time to save your work or download the project at this point from http://www.phptr.com/essential/flash/shelley/ shelley1-9.html.

# ◆ Texture Fills and Transparency

Now that you have created the basic shapes for the page, it is time to modify some of the fills and create some textures.

## Creating New Fill for Circles

Looking back at the page, you can see that the circles under the links appear to be spheres rather than the flat gray circles we have. We need to create the fill.

1. Select the Paint Bucket.

2. Click on the Fill Color button. Select the Color dialog button.

3. Click on the Gradient tab in the Color dialog box.

4. We are going to create a new Radial Fill. Click on the second image, a small round one, under the Gradient tab.

5. Look at Figure 1–54. Click on the right-hand color marker, shown in the image with the cursor on it. Change the RGB to 0, 102, 102.

6. Click New and close the dialog box by clicking on the X in the upper-right corner.

## Changing Fill of Circles

We've created the new fill for our circles, so let's use it.

1. Choose Edit→Edit Symbols.

2. Click on the Symbol List button in the top-right corner above the scene window (see Figure 1–55). Select the Link Circle.

3. Choose the Paint Bucket tool. The gradient fill you just created should be selected by default, but if it isn't, click on the fill at the bottom right of the palette and select it.

4. Deselect the circle. This will make it easier to see how the fill looks as it is being applied.

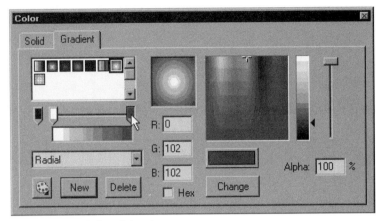

**FIGURE 1–54** Color dialog box

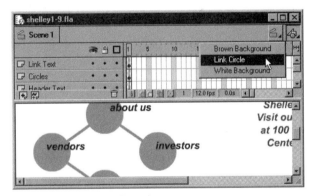

**FIGURE 1–55** Symbol List button

5. Click on the circle near the upper-right corner with the Paint Bucket to apply the fill. Make sure the Lock Fill option button is off.

6. Choose Edit→Edit Movie.

7. Since we made the circle a symbol, we don't need to repeat the process seven times. Changing the symbol's properties changed it for all the instances of that symbol.

**NOTE**
This would be a good time to save your work or download the project at this point from http://www.phptr.com/essential/flash/shelley/shelley1-10.html.

## Creating and Modifying the Transparent Circle

You have changed the circle fill. You still need to create a new gradient with transparency and use it for the last shape on the page. Let's start with creating the shape we need.

1. Click on the Address Text layer. If you haven't moved the address text over to the right, do so now. Figure 1–53 shows where it needs to go.

2. Hide the other layers.

3. We need to create the transparent gradient fill. Change to the Paint Bucket, click on the Fill Color, and open the Color dialog box. Select the Gradient tab.

4. Click on the gradient we created earlier. Click on the color marker on the right, as shown in Figure 1–56.

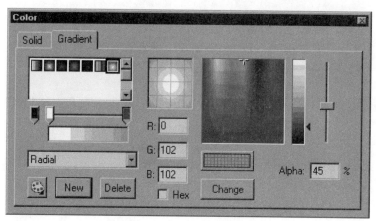

FIGURE 1–56 Color dialog box

5. Change the Alpha value to 45%.

6. Click on the marker on the left representing the white color and change its Alpha to 45%.

7. Click New and close the dialog box.

8. Choose the Oval tool. Set the line color to transparent by clicking on the Color palette and selecting the empty square on the upper left. The fill should be the gradient

you just created (see Figure 1–57). If it is not the correct fill, click on the Palette button and choose it from the bottom of the Palette dialog.

**FIGURE 1–57** Oval settings

9. Draw an oval around the text. Notice the transparency. Don't worry if it isn't perfectly placed. Just use the Arrow to move it and the Arrow with the Scale option to resize it (see Figure 1–58).

**FIGURE 1–58** Oval over the address text

10. Click on the top layer, Link Text.

11. Create a new layer and name it "Address Sphere." Select the oval and choose Edit→Cut. Now click on the newly created Sphere layer and choose Edit→Paste in Place. If necessary, turn off Snap and move the oval.

**NOTE**
This would be a good time to save your work or download the project at this point from http://www.phptr.com/essential/flash/shelley/shelley1-11.html.

# ◆ Importing Graphics

The last item you need for the homepage is the photo of the new Shelley office. You can download an image from the Web to use for importing to the page at http://www.phptr.com/essential/flash/shelley/misc/office.jpg.

## Importing an Image

1.  Choose Show All from the Layer menu.

2.  Select the top layer, Address Sphere.

3.  Create a new top layer and call it "Office Photo."

4.  Make sure this new layer is currently selected. Choose File→Import.

5.  Choose the image file you wish to use. The one used on the sample site may be downloaded from http://www.phptr.com/essential/flash/shelley/misc/office.jpg. Click OK.

6.  Use the Arrow tool to move the image to the appropriate location. You can resize the image using the handles with the Scale option selected.

## Changing the Photo Settings

1.  If the Library dialog box is not opened, choose Window→Library to open it.

2.  Locate the photo you just imported and select it.

3.  Choose Properties from the Options menu. This opens the Bitmap Properties dialog box for the image.

4.  Uncheck the Use Imported JPEG Data box (see Figure 1–59).

5.  Set the Quality to 100. Click OK.

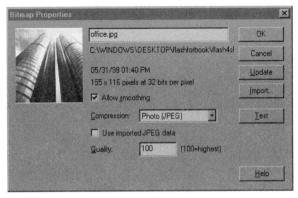

**FIGURE 1–59** Bitmap Properties dialog box

**NOTE**
This would be a good time to save your work or download the project at this point from http://www.phptr.com/essential/flash/shelley/ shelley1-12.html.

## RECAP

In this chapter you learned how to:
- Create a new movie and modify its properties
- Draw simple shapes
- Scale, modify, and move simple shapes
- Import graphics

## ADVANCED PROJECTS

1. Close the current Shelley movie and open a new movie.

2. Draw some simple lines and shapes. Try changing the options, such as color, line style, and thickness. Select them and change their color, size, and styles with the Text tool. Use the Arrow to add curves to their edges. Use the Arrow with the Scale and Rotate options to further modify them.

3.  Create some text objects with different fonts, sizes, and colors. Don't forget to choose the menu option View→ Antialias Text!

4.  Practice selecting and deselecting objects with the Arrow pointer.

5.  Draw and modify several shapes and use the Edit→Undo option repeatedly to return them to their original state.

6.  Import various images of different types.

7.  Use the Arrow tool with the Scale option. Notice how imported raster images such as GIFs, JPEGs, and BMPs look very blurry when they are scaled.

You've created all the graphics for the basic page. Chapter 2, "Animating the Page," will show you how to animate the pieces of this page.

# 2 Animating the Page

## IN THIS CHAPTER

- Timelines and Frames
- Movement Tweening
- Shape Tweening
- Fading
- Recap
- Advanced Projects

*You have totally re-created the Shelley Biotech homepage graphics with Flash. Now comes the fun part: animating it!*

*In this chapter you will learn the basic concepts you need to create animation in Flash movies. You will gain an understanding of what an animation is, the difference between the speed and the length of your animation, and what interface elements the Flash editor contains to help you create and control your animation.*

## ◆ Timelines and Frames

Because we will be animating so many different objects, we need to do some additional organization. You can download the

**41**

current project at http://www.phptr.com/essential/flash/shelley/ shelley1-12.html (see Figure 2–1).

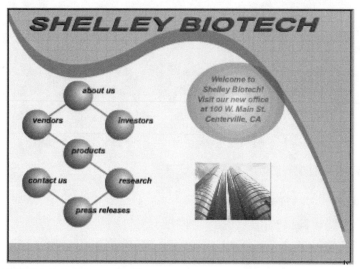

**FIGURE 2–1** Current Shelley page

### Creating the Link Text Symbol

1. Use the Arrow and hold down the Shift key to select the seven text links: about us, vendors, investors, products, contact us, research, and press releases.

2. Choose Modify→Group.

3. Choose Insert→Convert to Symbol.

4. Name the new symbol "Link Text" and leave it as a graphic. Click OK.

### Creating the Logo Layer

The lines connecting the spheres need to be moved to their own layer. To do this:

1. Select the top layer in the layer list and click on the Add Layer button, shown in Figure 2–2. This is another way to add new layers.

2. Name the new layer "Logo."

3. If necessary, move the link text over the spheres.

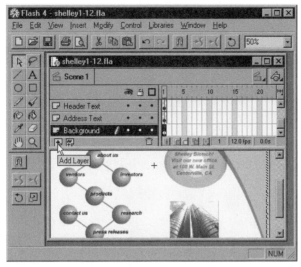

**FIGURE 2–2** Flash interface with the Add Layer button

**4.** Click on one of the lines. This will select all the lines and spheres, because we grouped them earlier.

**5.** Choose Modify→Ungroup.

**6.** Choose Edit→Deselect All.

**7.** Use the Arrow and the Shift key to select all the lines.

**8.** Choose Edit→Cut.

**9.** Select the Logo layer.

**10.** Choose Edit→Paste in Place. You have now moved the lines to the new layer. They are in front of the spheres, but we'll be moving them in a moment.

**11.** With the lines still selected, choose Modify→Group.

**12.** Finally, make the lines into a symbol by selecting Insert→ Convert to Symbol. Name this symbol "Lines" and leave it as a graphic (see Figure 2–3). Click OK.

**NOTE**
This would be a good time to save your work or download the project at this point from http://www.phptr.com/essential/flash/shelley/ shelley2-1.html.

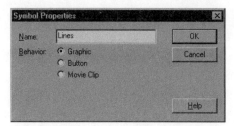

**FIGURE 2–3** Symbol Properties dialog box

## Adding an Additional Background Layer

Both the white and the brown curves making up the background will be animated. We need a separate layer for each.

1. Click on the Background layer.

2. Choose Insert Layer from the Layer menu. This will place a new layer immediately above the Background layer.

3. Rename this "Background 1."

4. Select the white curve. Choose Edit→Cut.

5. Select the Background 1 layer and choose Edit→Paste in Place.

6. Rename the original Background layer "Background 2."

## Creating Some Layers for the Circles

The last organizational change you need to make involves moving each of the seven spheres to separate layers.

1. Create the following new layers: Press Releases, Research, Contact Us, Investors, Vendors, About Us, Products.

2. For each of the corresponding spheres, select it, choose Edit→Cut, click on the appropriate new layer (according to the accompanying text link), and choose Edit→Paste in Place.

3. When all the spheres have been moved, select the Circles layer and choose Delete Layer from the Layer menu.

Select and drag the layers up and down to move them. Put your layers in the following order, from top to bottom:

1. **Header Text.** This is the Shelley Biotech banner and associated shadow.

2. **Link Text.**

3. **Address Text.**

4. **Address Sphere.** This is the sphere under the Address Text.

5. **Office Photo.**

6. **Link Sphere layers.** Each of the seven spheres should be in a separate layer.

7. **Logo.** This consists of the seven lines that connect the link spheres.

8. **Background 1.** The white curve.

9. **Background 2.** The brown curve.

**NOTE**

This would be a good time to save your work or download the project at this point from http://www.phptr.com/essential/flash/shelley/shelley2-2.html.

## Frames and Animation

One of the most important aspects of a Flash movie is the animation, which is nothing more than a series of still images, displayed over time. Each of these still images is called a *frame*. The speed at which the frames are displayed is controlled by the fps (frames per second) setting in Flash. A setting of 12 fps, which is the default setting, means that 12 frames will be displayed every second.

There are two ways to change the fps value:

1. Double-click the fps box, which is located just below the timeline (see Figure 2–4).

2. Choose the menu option Modify→Movie.

Both of these open the Movie Properties dialog box (see Figure 2–5). The first blank in this dialog box contains the frame rate. A rate between 8 and 15 is recommended. This range allows

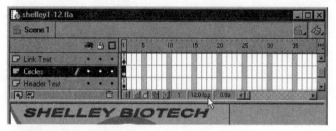

**FIGURE 2–4** The fps box

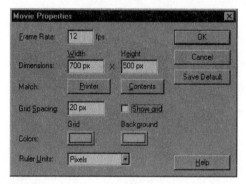

**FIGURE 2–5** The Movie Properties dialog box. The fps rate can be changed here.

relatively speedy processing of the animation while retaining smoothness of motion. For our animation, make sure the value is set at 12.

## Tweening and Keyframes

Before the advent of computers, cartoon animators had to draw each frame of an animation. Although you can do that with Flash, you are provided with a time-saving method of animation that requires you to create only the most important frames. Flash creates the intermediate frames for you. This is called *tweening*. Using tweening, you create only special frames, called *keyframes*, to serve as turning points during an animation, and Flash fills in the gaps. For example, if you wanted to animate an object moving to the right, hitting the edge of the screen, and moving left, you would only have to create three keyframes, and tell Flash to do the rest.

### Adding Keyframes to the Shelley Biotech Page

We can now put in place the keyframes we will need for the Shelley page.

1. Open the latest version of the Shelley file. This can be downloaded from http://www.phptr.com/essential/flash/shelley/shelley2-2.html.

2. We now need to select the 30th frame of all the layers. To do this, click and hold on the frame area at the 30 frame mark of the top layer and drag downward until all the layers are selected (see Figure 2–6).

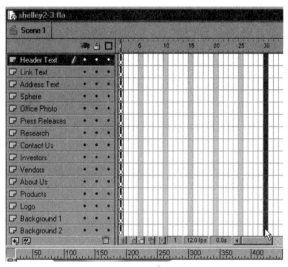

**FIGURE 2–6** Selecting the 30th frame of all the layers

3. Choose Insert→Keyframe.

4. The solid black circles indicate keyframe locations. Each layer should now have two, located at zero and 30. Figure 2–7 shows a layer with two keyframes.

**FIGURE 2–7** Layer with two keyframes

**NOTE**

This would be a good time to save your work or download the project at this point from http://www.phptr.com/essential/flash/shelley/ shelley2-3.html.

---

If you click on the first or last keyframe or any frame in between, you will notice that nothing changes. Two things still need to be done: First, you select a keyframe and make some change to the graphic at that point. Then you must tell Flash what kind of tweening to use. Flash can tween the movement of an object as well as its shape and color. The next section will show you how to animate the graphics on this page.

One final note: The graphics we created in Chapter 1, "The Basics," are the final product of the animation. We will be working backward and modifying the first keyframe, while leaving the last one alone. To get a clearer picture of this, go look at the finished product at http://www.phptr.com/essential/flash/shelley/ new/ and notice that the page ends up looking like our current file, but looks totally different when you first see it.

## ◆ Movement Tweening

The animation you will perform more than any other will be *movement tweening*. This consists of giving an object a starting and an ending location and letting Flash interpolate the frames in between. Movement tweening also interpolates on the basis of object size and rotation.

### Animating the Tan Background Curve

Figure 2–8 shows the path of this object. Only the outlines of the object are shown. In Flash, this view is called *onion-skinning*.

1.  Begin by selecting the Background 2 layer and hiding all the others, using the Layer menu.

2.  Click on the first keyframe.

3.  Open the Inspector window by choosing Window→ Inspectors→Object.

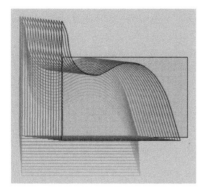

**FIGURE 2–8** The animated path of the tan background object. The darker lines indicate the most recent events.

4. You will be moving the curve partly off the movie window. To allow you to see it, choose View→Work Area. You may also find it useful to use the Zoom drop-down box along the top toolbar and set it to 50%.

5. Change to the Arrow tool. Select the curve and move it to the left and down, as shown in Figure 2–9.

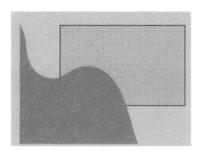

**FIGURE 2–9** Tan curve location at first keyframe

6. Add a keyframe at 14 by clicking at the 14 mark on the layer and selecting Insert→Keyframe.

7. Click on this new keyframe.

8. Move the curve up, as shown in Figure 2–10.

9. Click on a frame anywhere between the first and second keyframe. Choose Modify→Frame to open the Frame Properties

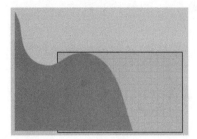

**FIGURE 2–10** Tan curve location at second keyframe

dialog box. You can also right-click (PC) or Ctrl-click (Mac) on the frame and select Properties from the pop-up menu.

**10.** Select the Tweening tab on this dialog box. Choose Motion from the drop-down list. Tween scaling should be checked, and Rotate should be Automatic. The Easing slider should be centered (see Figure 2–11). Click OK.

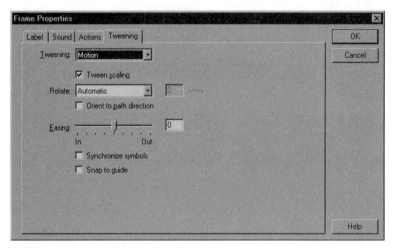

**FIGURE 2–11** Frame Properties dialog box

**11.** Click on a frame between the second and third keyframes, and repeat step 9.

**12.** To test your animation, select the first keyframe and press the Enter key.

**NOTE**

This would be a good time to save your work or download the project at this point from http://www.phptr.com/essential/flash/shelley/shelley2-4.html.

## A Quick Word about Onion-Skinning

Flash has a very nice feature that allows you to see the stages of an animated object over time. This is known as an *onion-skin* view. It displays the graphic in each frame at the same time, giving you a picture of the path it is taking. The first frames are fainter than the later frames. To use it, select the Onion Skin button, shown selected at the bottom of Figure 2–12. This image also shows the Onion Skin Markers on the Timeline. The color changes over time, with the faintest images representing the early frames. Turn it off by clicking on the Onion Skin button again. If you only wish to see the outlines, click on the Onion Skin Outlines button.

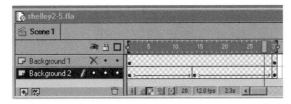

**FIGURE 2–12** Onion Skin markers on the Timeline

## Animating the Link Spheres

The link spheres will start out fairly large and centered on the one in the center, the Products sphere. They will shrink and move to the appropriate places. They will also fade in.

1. Begin by selecting the Products Sphere layer and hiding all the others by choosing Hide Others from the Layers Menu.

2. Click on the red X next to the names of the other six link sphere layers to make them appear. You should now see seven spheres against the tan background (see Figure 2–13).

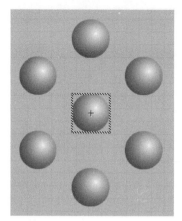

**FIGURE 2–13** Link spheres

**3.** Select the 15<sup>th</sup> frame on each of these layers and choose Insert→Keyframe. You can select them all at once if you click and hold on the 15<sup>th</sup> frame of the topmost sphere layer and drag down across the rest of the sphere layers. When you insert the keyframe it will be inserted in all the selected layers (see Figure 2–14).

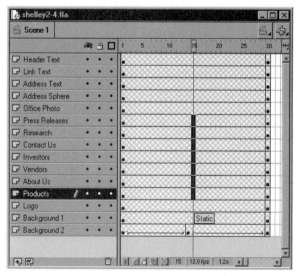

**FIGURE 2–14** Inserting a keyframe into several layers at once

4. Select the Products layer. The center sphere should now be selected.

5. Drag the Products layer below the other sphere layers.

6. Click on the first keyframe of the Products layer, located at frame 1. The sphere in this layer should be selected.

7. Open the Object Inspector by choosing Window→ Inspectors→Object.

8. Click in the Use Center Point check box and change the Width (w) and Height (h) each to 300 (see Figure 2–15). Click Apply.

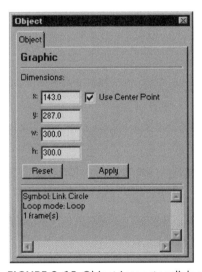

**FIGURE 2–15** Object Inspector dialog box

9. Make sure the first keyframe is still the current one. Use the Arrow and Shift key and select all the spheres.

10. Click on the first keyframe. Using the Arrow and Shift key, select the six outer spheres. Do not select the middle sphere.

11. Choose Modify→Align and use the settings shown in Figure 2–16. Click OK. This will make all the spheres 300 pixels x 300 pixels and centered, so only one will be visible, with the rest stacked under it.

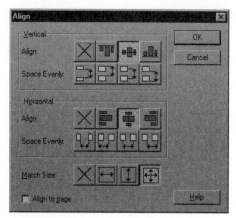

**FIGURE 2–16** Align dialog box

12. For each of the seven link sphere layers, click on a frame anywhere between the first and second keyframe. You can select all the layers at once by clicking on a frame of the top link sphere layer and dragging downward. Choose Modify→Frame to open the Frame Properties dialog box. You can also right-click (PC) or Ctrl-click (Mac) and select Properties from the pop-up menu.

13. Select the Tweening tab on this dialog box. Choose Motion from the drop-down list. Tween scaling should be checked, and Rotate should be Automatic. The Easing slider should be centered. Click OK.

14. The Instance Properties for the first keyframe for each of the seven spheres need to be changed. Click on the Products layer and hide the others. Select the first keyframe.

15. Select the link sphere in this layer and choose Modify→ Instance.

16. Change the Behavior to Button (see Figure 2–17). Click OK.

17. Repeat steps 14–16 for the other six sphere layers.

18. To see the results, press Enter. All the spheres should start out large and then should shrink while moving to their final locations. The animation should continue for another 15 seconds after the spheres quit moving.

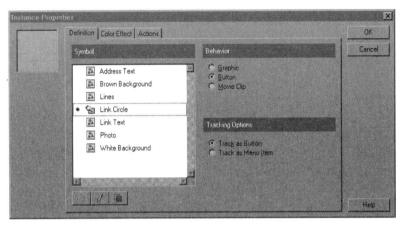

**FIGURE 2–17** Instance Properties dialog box

**NOTE**

This would be a good time to save your work or download the project at this point from http://www.phptr.com/essential/flash/shelley/shelley2-5.html.

## Animating the Address Text

Let's make the address text really large when the animation begins. In the section on fading, you will learn how to change its color to blend with the background and then change to its final green color. Figure 2–18 shows the onion-skinned path of this object.

1. Choose Show All from the Layer menu.

2. Click on the first keyframe of any layer.

3. Select View→Work Area. Use the Zoom Control and change the zoom to 50%.

4. With the Arrow, select the address text. Use the Layer menu to hide all the layers except for the Address layer. Click on the red X next to the Background 2 layer to make it visible also.

5. We need to turn the address text into a symbol. Make sure you are on the first keyframe with the Address Text

**FIGURE 2–18** Onion-skin view of address text animation

selected and choose Insert→Convert to Symbol. Name it "Address Text" and click OK.

6. Click on the last keyframe on the Address Text layer and choose Insert→Clear Keyframe.

7. Now put a keyframe back at this location by choosing Insert→Keyframe. The Address Text symbol we just created will now be present.

8. Select the first keyframe of the Address Text layer and select the text.

9. Click on the Scale button. Using the handles or Object Inspector, stretch the address text until it is approximately 1000 pixels wide and 1060 pixels high. Reposition and resize until the word "Shelley" is located on top of the visible part of the tan curve (see Figure 2–19). No other words should overlap the part of the tan curve located on the page area.

10. Click on a frame between the two keyframes on the Address Text layer. Select Modify→Frame.

11. Select the Tweening tab on this dialog box. Choose Motion from the drop-down list. Tween scaling should be checked, and Rotate should be Automatic. The Easing slider should be centered. Click OK.

12. To see the results, click on the first keyframe and press Enter.

**FIGURE 2–19** Address text stretched and moved

**NOTE**

This would be a good time to save your work or download the project at this point from http://www.phptr.com/essential/flash/shelley/shelley2-6.html.

## Animating the Text Links

The text links will be very small and on the right side of the screen, then grow in size and move left. Figure 2–20 shows the onion-skinned path of these objects.

**FIGURE 2–20** Onion-skin view of text links with page border shown

1. Begin by selecting the Link Text layer and hiding all the others, using the Layer menu.

2. Click on the first keyframe and select the links.

3.  Open the Inspector window and resize the group of links to approximately 40 pixels x 40 pixels and move it to an X, Y location of (500, 250). Click Apply.

4.  Click on a frame between the two keyframes on the Link Text layer. Select Modify→Frame.

5.  Select the Tweening tab on this dialog box. Choose Motion from the drop-down list. Tween scaling should be checked, and Rotate should be Automatic. The Easing slider should be centered. Click OK.

6.  To see the results, press Enter.

---

**NOTE**

This would be a good time to save your work or download the project at this point from http://www.phptr.com/essential/flash/shelley/shelley2-7.html.

---

### Animating the Header Text

Figure 2–21 shows the onion-skinned path of this object.

**FIGURE 2–21** Onion-skin view of header text with page border shown

1.  Begin by selecting the Header Text layer and hiding all the others using the Layer menu.

2.  Click on the first keyframe and select the header.

3.  Open the Inspector window. Resize the link object to approximately 130 pixels x 10 pixels and move it to an X, Y location of (630, 90).

4.  Click on a frame between the two keyframes on the Header Text layer. Select Modify→Frame.

5. Select the Tweening tab on this dialog box. Choose Motion from the drop-down list. Tween scaling should be checked, and Rotate should be Automatic. The Easing slider should be centered. Click OK.

6. To see the results, press Enter.

**NOTE**
This would be a good time to save your work or download the project at this point from http://www.phptr.com/essential/flash/shelley/shelley2-8.html.

If you haven't viewed the entire page animation already, select Show All from the Layer menu. Press Enter. You have now added all the motion tweening to the page.

## ◆ Shape Tweening

Shape tweening animation is used when you need to change or morph one shape into another. The shape and the color shifts gradually from the beginning graphic to the final one. As in motion tweening, Flash will interpolate the intermediate frames for you.

In the Shelley Biotech page, only one object undergoes shape tweening. This is the semitransparent egg-shaped sphere underneath the address text. We will make it start out as a large S and morph into the sphere.

### Creating the Beginning S Shape

Now, we need to create an S shape.

1. Select the Address Sphere layer and drag it to the top of the layer list. Hide the other layers.

2. Click on the first keyframe of the Sphere layer.

3. Select the oval shape in this keyframe and delete it with Edit→Clear or the Delete key.

4. Change to the Text tool. Set the font to Arial, the color to black, the size to 72, and click on both Bold and Italic.

5. Click on the scene and type an uppercase S.

6. Open the Object Inspector by choosing Window→Inspectors→Object.

7. Open the Inspector window. Resize the link object to approximately 30 by 155 pixels and to move it to an X, Y location of (615, 14). Make sure Use Center Point is unchecked!

8. Choose Modify→Break Apart. This will allow us to apply a gradient fill to the S.

9. We should make the S have the same colors as the final sphere it will become. Change to the Paint Bucket. Select the gradient fill from the Color palette that was used to fill the link spheres (see Figure 2–22).

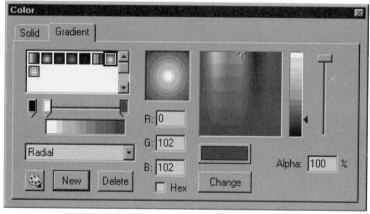

**FIGURE 2–22** Gradient tab of Color dialog box

10. Click on the S shape somewhere near the center. You may need to zoom out to accomplish this more easily, using the Zoom Control on the top toolbar.

11. Click on the red X next to the Header Text layer to make it visible. Make sure the S is covering the first letter of the header, as shown in Figure 2–23, by selecting it and using the Scale option with the Arrow.

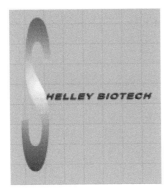

**FIGURE 2–23** S shape

Now that we have our starting and ending shapes, we can perform shape tweening and let Flash fill in the frames between them.

### Applying Shape Tweening to the S

1.  Hide the Header Text layer and all other layers except for the Address Sphere layer.

2.  Click on any frame between the starting and ending keyframes.

3.  Choose Modify→Frame and select the Tweening tab.

4.  Choose Shape Tweening with the Blend Type of Distributive, and move the Easing slider all the way over to the left (see Figure 2–24). Moving the Easing slider left makes the shape more S-shaped than circular.

5.  Press Enter to view the shape tweening.

**NOTE**
This would be a good time to save your work or download the project at this point from http://www.phptr.com/essential/flash/shelley/ shelley2-9.html.

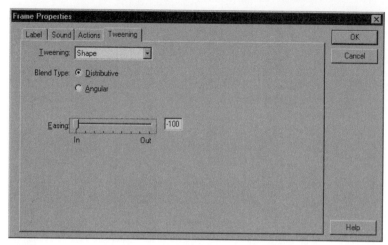

**FIGURE 2–24** Tweening tab of Frame Properties dialog box

## Adding Shape Hints

*Shape hints* are markers you place on the beginning and ending shapes in a shape tweening to tell Flash how to proceed in the frames between the two keyframes. When you create a shape hint, Flash puts a small labeled circle on the image at both the first and second keyframes. You can use the Arrow to move these markers. If you place the marker at the top of the image in the first keyframe, and at the bottom of the image in the second, the image will appear to turn itself inside out, with the top migrating toward the bottom during the animation.

1. Select the first keyframe in the Address Sphere layer and zoom in 200%.

2. Choose Modify→Transform→Add Shape Hints. A small red circle with the letter "a" in it appears. Use the Arrow to move it away from the S.

3. Add two more shape hints, b and c, and move them so all three are visible.

4. Move the letters to the locations shown in Figure 2–25.

5. Click on the last keyframe. Matching letters are stacked in the center of the oval. Move them to the locations shown in Figure 2–26.

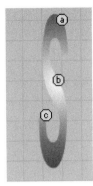

**FIGURE 2–25** Shape hints correctly placed on the S graphic

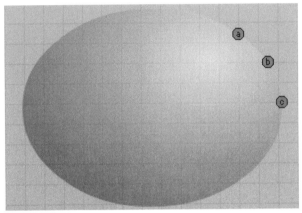

**FIGURE 2–26** Shape hints correctly placed on the transparent oval

6. Press Enter to see the result of the shape hint influence on the shape tweening.

7. To hide the shape hints from the view, uncheck View→ Show Shape Hints.

**NOTE**

This would be a good time to save your work or download the project at this point from http://www.phptr.com/essential/flash/shelley/shelley2-10.html.

If you make all the layers visible at this point and animate them, you'll notice that the page is rather cluttered. We will fix that in the next section.

# ◆ Fading

Now all that remains to be done is to apply some fading to the beginning keyframes of some of the images. This will help to clean up much of the clutter you see when you view the entire animation.

## Fading in the White Background

The white background layer is nice for the final frame of the animation, but is a bit distracting while the animation is taking place. Let's make it fade in.

1. We made the white background a symbol in Chapter 1. This allows us to modify its Instance Properties. Select the Background 1 layer and hide all the rest.

2. Click on the first keyframe.

3. With the Arrow, select the white curve. Choose Modify→ Instance. Double-clicking on the white curve will also open this dialog box.

4. Click on the Color Effect tab.

5. Choose Alpha from the drop-down list and set the percentage to zero by moving the slider to the left or typing in the text box (see Figure 2–27). Click OK.

6. Click on a frame between the two keyframes on the Background 1 layer. Select Modify→Frame.

7. Select the Tweening tab on this dialog box. Choose Motion from the drop-down list. Tween scaling should be checked, and Rotate should be Automatic. The Easing slider should be centered. Click OK.

8. To see the results, press Enter.

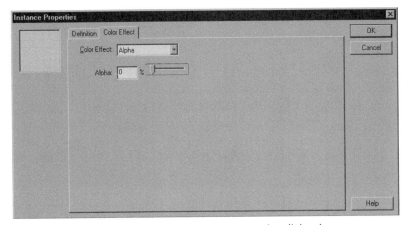

**FIGURE 2–27** Color Effect tab of Instance Properties dialog box

**NOTE**

This would be a good time to save your work or download the project at this point from http://www.phptr.com/essential/flash/shelley/shelley2-11.html.

## Fading in the Office Photo

The office photo will also fade in. The procedure is basically the same as before, except that the fade-in will begin at the 15th frame.

1. Select the Office Photo layer and hide all the rest.

2. Click on the first keyframe.

3. With the Arrow, select the photo.

4. We need to make the photo a symbol so we can modify its transparency. Choose Insert→Convert to Symbol. Name it "Photo" and click OK.

5. Click on the keyframe at 30 and choose Insert→Clear Keyframe. This will remove the keyframe at 30 that does not have the Photo symbol in it. The photo in this frame was not the Photo symbol you created in step 4. To create the fade effect, it must be the same symbol.

6. Now add a keyframe to 30 again by choosing Insert→ Keyframe. This time the photo image will be the Photo symbol you created.

7. Click on the first keyframe again. Select the photo.

8. Choose Modify→Instance. Double-clicking on the photo will also open this dialog box.

9. Click on the Color Effect tab.

10. Choose Alpha from the drop-down list and set the percentage to zero by moving the slider to the left or typing in the text box. Click OK.

11. Click on the 15$^{th}$ frame and choose Insert→Keyframe.

12. Click on a frame between the second and third keyframes on the Office Photo layer. Select Modify→Frame.

13. Select the Tweening tab on this dialog box. Choose Motion from the drop-down list. Tween scaling should be checked, and Rotate should be Automatic. The Easing slider should be centered. Click OK.

14. Press Enter to see the result. The fade-in begins at the 15$^{th}$ frame and finishes at the 30$^{th}$.

**NOTE**

This would be a good time to save your work or download the project at this point from http://www.phptr.com/essential/flash/shelley/ shelley2-12.html.

## Fading in the Logo Lines

The lines connecting the link spheres should also be faded in.

1. Select the Logo layer and hide all the rest.

2. Click on the first keyframe.

3. With the Arrow, select the lines. Choose Modify→Instance. Double-clicking on the lines will also open this dialog box.

4. Click on the Color Effect tab.

5. Choose Alpha from the drop-down list and set the percentage to zero by moving the slider to the left or typing in the text box. Click OK.

6. Click on a frame between the two keyframes on the Logo Lines layer. Select Modify→Frame.

7. Select the Tweening tab on this dialog box. Choose Motion from the drop-down list. Tween scaling should be checked, and Rotate should be Automatic. The Easing slider should be centered. Click OK.

8. To see the results, press Enter.

---

**NOTE**
This would be a good time to save your work or download the project at this point from http://www.phptr.com/essential/flash/shelley/shelley2-13.html.

---

## Changing the Color of the Text Links

Instead of fading in the text links, the color will change. The color will start out the same as the background and then will change to black. This will make the links stand out a bit more than if they were faded in.

1. Select the Link Text layer and hide all the rest.

2. Click on the first keyframe.

3. With the Arrow, select the links. Choose Modify→ Instance. Double-clicking on the lines will also open this dialog box.

4. Click on the Color Effect tab.

5. Choose Tint from the drop-down list and set the Tint Amount percentage to 100 by moving the slider to the right or entering the amount in the text box.

6. Change the color values to a red of 204, green of 204, and blue of 153, as shown in Figure 2–28. Click OK.

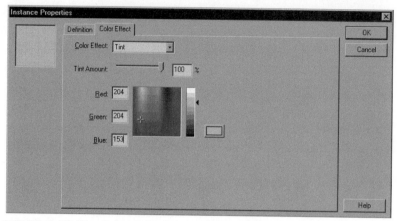

**FIGURE 2–28** The Color dialog box with the RGB set appropriately

**7.** To see the results, press Enter.

**NOTE**
This would be a good time to save your work or download the project at this point from http://www.phptr.com/essential/flash/shelley/shelley2-14.html.

## Fading in the Link Spheres

The link spheres already have a blurred look when they are animated. We can enhance this by making each fade in.

**1.** Select one of the seven link sphere layers and hide the rest.

**2.** Click on the first keyframe.

**3.** With the Arrow Image, select the link sphere. Choose Modify→Instance.

**4.** Click on the Color Effect tab.

**5.** Choose Alpha from the drop-down list and set the percentage to zero by moving the slider to the left or typing in the text box. Click OK.

6. The spheres already have motion tweening, so you will not need to add it. Repeat this procedure for each of the other six link spheres.

7. To see the results, press Enter.

**NOTE**

This would be a good time to save your work or download the project at this point from http://www.phptr.com/essential/flash/shelley/shelley2-15.html.

## Changing the Color of the Address Text

1. Select the Address Text layer and hide the others.

2. Click on the first keyframe.

3. With the Arrow, select the address text. Choose Modify→ Instance. Double-clicking on the text will also open this dialog box.

4. Click on the Color Effect tab.

5. Choose Tint from the drop-down list and set the Tint Amount percentage to 100 by moving the slider to the right or entering the amount in the text box.

6. Change the color values to a red of 204, green of 204, and blue of 153, as shown in Figure 2–29. Click OK.

7. To see the results, press Enter.

**NOTE**

This would be a good time to save your work or download the project at this point from http://www.phptr.com/essential/flash/shelley/shelley2-16.html.

You have created the graphics for the homepage and animated them. In the next chapter, "Making the Page Interactive,"

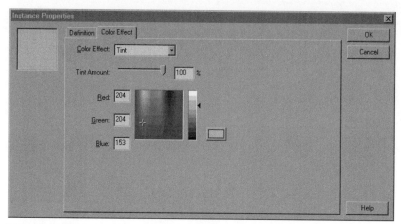

**FIGURE 2-29** Color Effect tab of Instance Properties dialog box

you will add buttons and links to make the page interactive, and we will examine symbols and buttons in depth.

## RECAP

In this chapter you learned how to:

- Create symbols and animate them
- Animate the color of symbols
- Animate symbols fading
- Morph shapes

## ADVANCED PROJECTS

1. In a new movie, create several layers with a graphic in each and turn these into symbols.

2. Create a layer with a different graphic at different keyframes.

3. Use shape tweening to morph one shape into another.

4. Try adding shape hints to control the morphing.

5. Animate the shapes so they appear to collide.

6. Use fading and color effects on the shapes before and after the collision.

# 3 Making the Page Interactive

## IN THIS CHAPTER

- Symbols
- Creating Buttons
- Button Actions
- Sound Effects
- Recap
- Advanced Projects

*The Shelley Biotech page has been created and animated, but it still lacks an important element that Flash offers: interactivity. We will start with a brief overview of symbols, important devices for creating interactivity. Then you will learn how to create buttons that will respond to mouse cursor actions. Finally, you'll learn how to add sound to your Flash movie.*

## ◆ Symbols

Flash *symbols* are graphic objects that are stored by Flash. What makes symbols so important is their reusability. When you create a symbol, you can use it over and over again without having to redraw it each time you need it. And if you decide to change it, you don't need to change each copy, or instance, of it; you can simply change the stored master symbol. Changing the master symbol changes all the instances of it in your Flash movie.

There are three types of symbols: graphics, buttons, and movie clips. Graphics are noninteractive images to which animation and sounds can be attached. Buttons are graphics that can also respond to mouse actions. Movie clips are entire Flash movies that can be reused inside other movies.

There are a few basic tasks you should know: how to create a symbol, how to interact with a symbol library, how to edit a symbol, and how to change its type.

### Creating Symbols

In the earlier chapters, we created many symbols. There are two ways to create a symbol. After you have created a graphic you want to convert, you can either choose the menu option Insert→Create Symbol or press the F8 key. Once you have created the symbol, it is automatically stored in the local library.

### Using the Library to Access Your Symbols

To see all the symbols you have in your movie, open the Library using the menu option Window→Library or Ctrl-L. You can see the Library window in Figure 3–1. The Library stores not only the symbols used in your movie, but also any other importable media you have used, such as sound files and bitmaps. You can change the type of media you are seeing in the Library with the toggle buttons at the top.

Each movie has a library associated with it, and Macromedia also ships with some media libraries, which are collections of sounds, buttons, movies, and prebuilt form elements for you to use in your own Flash applications. Unlike movie libraries, these libraries cannot be modified. To use items from these libraries, you must drag them onto your movie. They will then appear in your local library. You can access the Macromedia libraries under the menu item Libraries. These libraries cannot be modified.

### Editing Symbols

There are several ways to edit symbols. In the Library, you can select the symbol you wish to edit and pull up the Symbol menu by clicking on the Options button at the top right. The Symbol menu allows you to create, delete, modify, copy, and file symbols

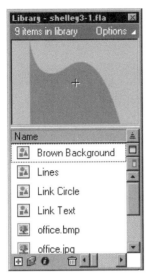

**FIGURE 3–1** Library dialog box

in subfolders for better organization. You can also choose Edit→Edit Symbols. Symbol editing mode allows you to change the appearance, animation, and actions associated with a symbol without having to change the movie in which the symbol appears. When you switch to symbol editing mode, the name of the symbol appears underneath the file name at the top of the movie. Figure 3–2 shows the symbol editing mode for the Brown Background symbol. Once you are in symbol editing mode, you can switch between symbols by using the Symbol List button at the top-right side of the window.

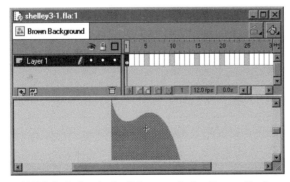

**FIGURE 3–2** Symbol editing mode for Brown Background symbol

## Changing Symbol Types

In this chapter, we will be turning some of the graphics we created previously into buttons. If a symbol has not been used in an animation, you can change its type with the Symbol Properties dialog box. Selecting the symbol in the Library, and choosing Properties from the Options menu in the Library dialog box, will access this dialog box. You can then change the type by clicking on the appropriate radio button, as seen in Figure 3–3.

**FIGURE 3–3** Symbol Properties dialog box

In Chapter 2, "Animating the Page," we used some of our symbols in an animation. This means that we will have to change the type in several places, unfortunately. Not only does the Symbol Property have to be changed, but the Instance Property will need to be changed for each keyframe in which the symbol is involved. If you're confused, don't worry; this will be clarified in the next section.

## ◆ Creating Buttons

Unlike symbols, buttons allow you to attach actions to them. This means that buttons can change colors, make sounds, and serve as links to new pages when they are pressed. All buttons have four special frames that can be assigned actions: Up, Over, Down, and Hit. These refer to mouse cursor locations. Up is the default state of the button when the cursor is not touching it. Over means the cursor is overlapping the button. Down is the same as Over, except that the mouse button is pressed. Hit is used to define an area around the button. We will learn how to add these properties in the next section.

Our seven Link Circle symbols need to act as buttons and load the particular page to which they refer. In Chapter 1, "The Basics," we created the Link Circle instances. Ordinarily, those would have been created as buttons initially. We didn't do this because we were focusing on creating the graphics, so we will convert them into buttons now. Converting them at this point requires several steps.

## Changing the Link Circle Symbol's Properties

The Link Circle is now a graphic symbol. Let's start by changing it to a button.

1. Open the Library dialog box by selecting Window→Library.

2. In the scroll-down list, select the Link Circle symbol. Choose Properties from the Options menu (see Figure 3–4).

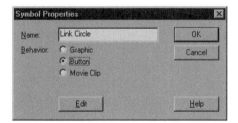

**FIGURE 3–4** Symbol Properties dialog box

3. Change the behavior to Button and click OK.

## Changing the Instance Properties for the Link Spheres

1. Make sure you are in movie editing mode by choosing Edit→Edit Movie.

2. Select the Arrow tool.

3. Right-click (PC) or Ctrl-click (Mac) on the Products layer. Choose Hide Others from the Layer menu.

4. Click on the middle keyframe of the Products layer.

5. Click on the middle link sphere, which is the Products link sphere.

6. Choose Modify→Instance.

7. On the Definition tab, change the behavior to Button (see Figure 3–5). Click OK.

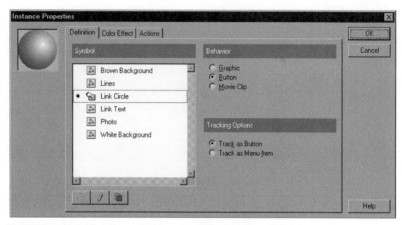

**FIGURE 3–5** Definition tab of Instance Properties dialog box

8. Click on the last keyframe of the Products layer.

9. Repeat steps 5–7 for this keyframe.

10. You must do this for the middle and last keyframes of the other six link spheres. Unfortunately, there is no easy way to do this all at once.

**NOTE**
This would be a good time to save your work or download the project at this point from http://www.phptr.com/essential/flash/shelley/shelley3-1.html.

By changing the spheres to buttons in the middle and last keyframes, and leaving the first keyframe as a graphic, we are telling Flash to treat them as buttons after the 15th keyframe and from then on. The point of this will become more obvious after we apply some button frame actions.

## Adding the Web Links to the Buttons

Now we can make the spheres link to the appropriate subpages when they are clicked on.

1. Click on the last keyframe.

2. Double-click on the about us link sphere, or select it and choose Modify→Instance. This will be the sphere closest to the top of the page.

3. Click on the Actions tab.

4. Click on the button with the plus sign and choose Get URL from the menu (see Figure 3–6).

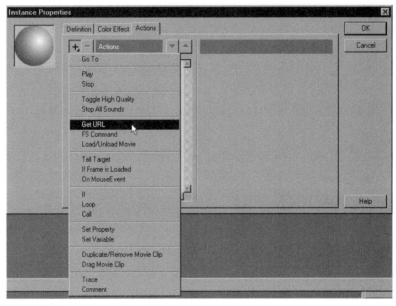

**FIGURE 3–6** Adding a Get URL action

5. Type the URL http://www.phptr.com/essential/flash/shelley/about.html in the box on the right (see Figure 3–7). Click OK.

6. Repeat this process for each of the link spheres, linking to the pages vendors.html, investors.html, products.html, contact.html, research.html, and press.html, as appropriate.

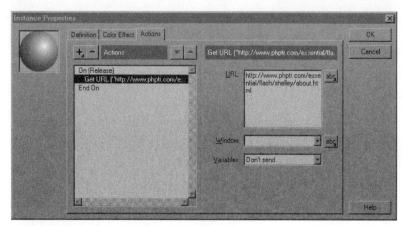

**FIGURE 3–7** Adding the URL to the action

**NOTE**

This would be a good time to save your work or download the project at this point from http://www.phptr.com/essential/flash/shelley/shelley3-2.html.

## Testing the Links

At this point, there is no easy way to test the URLs you have just added. You can tell whether or not a URL link exists, but you can't tell what the link is without actually publishing the movie or checking the Instance Properties for the buttons. To test to see whether a link exists, choose Control→Enable Buttons. As you move your mouse over the buttons in frames 15 to 30, the mouse cursor will change to a link hand cursor, as shown in Figure 3–8. When you are done, uncheck the Control→Enable Buttons option.

**FIGURE 3–8** The cursor changes to a hand cursor over the button

# ◆ Button Actions

Four actions are associated with each button. When you changed the symbol properties of the link sphere from type graphic to button, these four actions were added to the button's symbol editing window.

## Opening the Button Frame Action Window

When you turned the link sphere into a button, the four frame actions were added to it. To access them:

1. Open the Window→Library dialog box.

2. Scroll down and select the Link Circle symbol.

3. Click on the Options menu, as shown in Figure 3–9, and choose Edit. The four frames for our button are now visible.

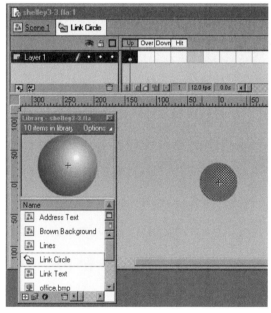

**FIGURE 3–9** The four button frames

4. Double-click on the Layer 1 label and change its name to "Action."

Fortunately, we will have to set the action only once for the link sphere symbol instead of setting it multiple times, once for each link sphere.

### Adding the Keyframes for Button Actions

The three actions we need to edit do not have keyframes. Let's add them.

1.  Click directly beneath the word "Over" in the Layer 1 timeline.

2.  Choose Insert→Keyframe. A small black dot should appear, as shown in Figure 3–10.

**FIGURE 3–10** Keyframe inserted at the Over frame

3.  Click directly beneath the word "Down" in the Layer 1 timeline.

4.  Choose Insert→Keyframe.

5.  Click directly beneath the word "Hit" in the Layer 1 timeline.

6.  Choose Insert→Keyframe. Your Layer 1 should now look like Figure 3–11.

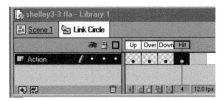

**FIGURE 3–11** All of the button keyframes inserted

To edit each frame, you will click on the keyframe below it. Each frame starts out looking like the beginning one. Let's make our button change when the mouse cursor is passed over it.

### Creating the Hit Frame

The Hit frame defines the area around the button that will respond as the link to mouse clicks. On the Shelley page, both the button and the text link to the right of it should be clickable.

1. You should be in symbol editing mode for the link sphere symbol The symbol name, "Link Sphere," should appear above the top toolbar.

2. Click on the Hit frame.

3. Choose the Rectangle tool. Select black for the line and fill colors, 1.0 for the line thickness, and Solid for the line style (see Figure 3–12).

**FIGURE 3–12** Rectangle settings

4. Draw a rectangle to the right of the link sphere, as shown in Figure 3–13.

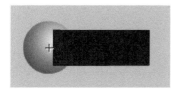

**FIGURE 3–13** Rectangle defining the hit area

**NOTE**

This would be a good time to save your work or download the project at this point from http://www.phptr.com/essential/flash/shelley/shelley3-3.html.

## Creating the Over Frame

We will change the appearance of the button when the mouse cursor runs over it.

1.  You should be in symbol editing mode for the Link Circle symbol. Your workspace should look like Figure 3–14.

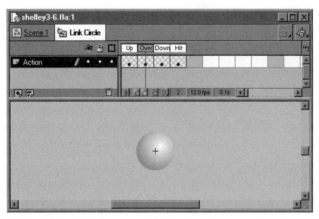

**FIGURE 3–14** Workspace with the Over frame selected

2.  We will create a new texture to fill this sphere. Select the Paint Bucket.

3.  Click on the Fill Color. Select the Color Edit button on the palette.

4.  Click on the Gradient tab on the Color dialog box.

5.  We are going to create a new Radial Fill. Click on the second image, a small round image, under the Gradient tab.

6.  Look at Figure 3–15. Click on the right-hand color marker. Change the RGB to 153, 153, 102.

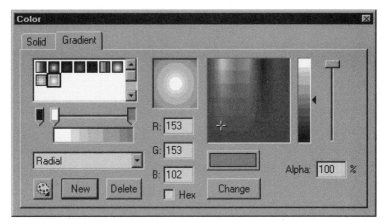

FIGURE 3–15 Color dialog box with Gradient tab selected

7. Click New and close the dialog box by clicking the X in the upper-right corner.

8. Select the Over frame.

9. Apply this fill to the Over keyframe using the Paint Bucket, clicking near the upper right of the button. It should look like the original link sphere, but with a tan color replacing the blue.

10. To check the change you just made, click on each of the keyframes. Notice that the Over and Hit frames are different from the other two.

**NOTE**
This would be a good time to save your work or download the project at this point from http://www.phptr.com/essential/flash/shelley/shelley3-4.html.

### Creating the Down Frame

This will change the appearance of the button when it is clicked.

1. You should be in symbol editing mode for the link sphere symbol.

2. We will create a new texture to fill this sphere with. Select the Paint Bucket.

3. Click on the Fill Color. Select the Color Edit button.

4. Click on the Gradient tab on the Color dialog box.

5. We are going to create a new Radial Fill. Click on the second image, a small round one, under the Gradient tab.

6. Look at Figure 3–16. Click on the left-hand color marker. Change the RGB to 255, 255, 255. Click on the right-hand color marker. Change the RGB to 0, 102, 102.

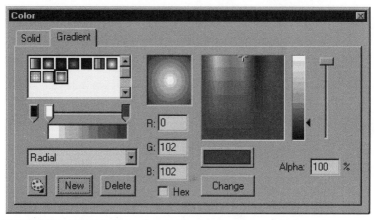

**FIGURE 3–16** Color dialog box with the Gradient tab selected

7. Click New and close the dialog box by clicking the X in the upper-right corner.

8. Select the Down keyframe and apply this fill using the Paint Bucket, clicking near the lower left of the button. The button should look like Figure 3–17.

9. To check the change you just made, click on each of the keyframes.

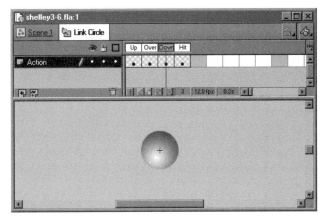

**FIGURE 3–17** Button appearance at the Down keyframe

**NOTE**
This would be a good time to save your work or download the project at this point from http://www.phptr.com/essential/flash/shelley/shelley3-5.html.

## Testing the Button Actions

The area of the button that will act as a link and respond to mouse actions is now defined. You can test the changes you just made.

1. Choose the menu option Edit→Edit Movie.

2. You are now presented with your current scene. Select Control→Enable Buttons.

3. Click on the last frame of your animation.

4. Move your mouse over the buttons and click on them to see the actions.

5. When you are through, uncheck the Control→Enable Buttons option.

# ◆ Sound Effects

Our buttons now respond to mouse motions and clicks. We can also add a sound to them that will play when they are clicked. Macromedia ships a library of sounds for your use. We will be using one of them, but first you will see how to add your own .wav file if you desire.

## Adding a Sound to the Library

First we need to add the button sound to the current Library. This will then allow us to add it to the button.

1. Open the Library window by choosing Window→Library.

2. Choose File→Import.

3. Select a sound file from your disk, such as a WAV (PC) or an AIFF (Mac).

4. The file now appears in your Library window.

## Using the Macromedia Sound Library

Using a sound from the Macromedia Sound Library is a bit trickier.

1. Open the Macromedia Sound Library by choosing the menu option Libraries→Sounds.

2. The window shown in Figure 3–18 will open.

FIGURE 3–18 Macromedia Sound Library dialog box

3. Preview the various sounds by clicking on the Play button, the arrow pointing to the right. We have to create a layer for the sound before we can add it to our button.

### Adding Sound to the Buttons

Adding sound to the buttons is done in symbol editing mode.

1. Scroll through the list in the Library dialog box and click on the Link Circle. Click on the Options button on the upper right of the dialog box and choose Edit. You are now in symbol editing mode.

2. You should see the frames we added earlier for the button actions. We need to add a new layer for the sound. Choose Insert→Layer.

3. Rename the new layer "Sounds" by double-clicking on its name and typing it in (see Figure 3–19).

**FIGURE 3–19** Sounds layer added to the Link Circle

4. Click under the Down frame on the Sounds layer and choose Insert→Keyframe (see Figure 3–20).

**FIGURE 3–20** Keyframe added to the Down frame of the Sounds layer

5. Drag the sound you wish to use from the library to the Link Circle symbol editing window. If you want to use

the Macromedia sound, you will drag from the Sounds Library. If you want to use a sound you imported to the Local Library, select and drag that one.

6. Double-click the Down keyframe. The Frame Properties dialog box will open.

7. To change the properties of this sound, click on the Sound tab in the Frame Properties dialog box, as shown in Figure 3–21. Click OK.

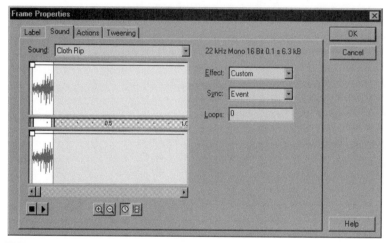

**FIGURE 3–21** Sound tab in the Frame Properties dialog box

**NOTE**
This would be a good time to save your work or download the project at this point from http://www.phptr.com/essential/flash/shelley/shelley3-6.html.

## Testing the Sound Effect

You should now have a sound when the buttons are clicked on. You can test this.

1. Choose the menu option Edit→Edit Movie.

2. You are now presented with your current scene. Select Control→Enable Buttons.

3. Click on the last frame of your animation.

4. Move your mouse over the buttons and click on them to see the actions and hear the sound.

5. When you are through, uncheck the Control→Enable Buttons option.

Congratulations! You have now added some basic interactivity and sound to the link buttons. This concludes the design and programming tasks needed for the Shelley project. In the next chapter, we will move on to publishing the page on the Web.

## RECAP

In this chapter you learned how to:
- Create and edit symbols
- Make buttons
- Add actions and sound effects to buttons

## ADVANCED PROJECTS

1. In a new movie, create several layers and use the Macromedia libraries to add symbols.

2. Open the symbol library for the current movie, and duplicate and rename a symbol. Change it to a button symbol.

3. Insert a Get URL action for this button.

4. Change to symbol editing mode for the new button. Insert keyframes and change the appearance of the button for Up, Over, and Down.

5. Add different sounds for Over and Down and test the button.

# 4 Publishing to the Web

## IN THIS CHAPTER

- Finishing Touches
- Publishing
- Preloading
- Detecting the Plug-In
- Web Server Settings
- Recap
- Advanced Projects

*Now that the homepage has been re-created with Flash, it's time to publish to the Web. We will start with a brief discussion of some production issues; you will need to make some decisions about how your homepage will be delivered to your audience. We will address some optimization issues. We will publish the homepage to the Web in several different formats and test them. Publishing options for your page will be discussed, and. we will add preloading and plug-in detection. Finally, we will mention some Web server issues.*

## ◆ Finishing Touches

Before we can publish our page, we need to make some decisions about the audience. Flash gives you many output options. From providing text links for all the links in your Flash Application to producing static or animated GIFs, Flash lets you create multimedia productions while still allowing you to provide content to visitors with older browsers, low bandwidth, and fewer colors on their machines.

## Deciding What Resolution to Use

The screen resolution dictates how large or small Web pages will appear. Someone with a screen resolution of 640 pixels by 480 pixels will see much less of a Web page than someone with a 1024 by 768 screen resolution.

Is your audience composed of many people who view the Web in 800 by 600 resolution? Or do you want to support the lowest common denominator, which might be 640 by 480? Flash has a nice feature that will allow your page to scale with the browser. To see what this means, look at Figures 4–1 and 4–2.These are screen shots of two browser windows on the same machine. The one in Figure 4–1 has simply been reduced in size. Notice that the entire page is still visible in both windows, despite the viewable size.

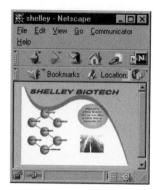

**FIGURE 4–1** Screen shot with browser window smaller

Your other option is to set the page as a fixed size. Viewers may need to scroll the browser window to view the entire page. This option is probably better when you are confident that your viewers are running in a higher resolution. See Figure 4–3 for an example of a tiny browser window with Flash set to display as a fixed size.

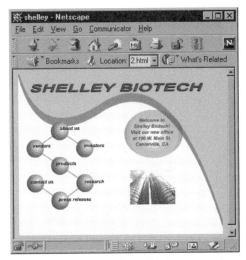

**FIGURE 4–2** Screen shot with browser window larger

**FIGURE 4–3** Screen shot with Flash set to display fixed size page

## Deciding Which Platforms to Use

Not all your visitors will view your site using Windows 98 with Internet Explorer 5. Some will use Macintoshes or Unix machines with Netscape Navigator. Some people will be using Lynx and will not be able to view your Flash movie at all. You need to decide which browsers you will support. The Flash plug-in is included with some browsers, has to be downloaded with others, and is not supported at all on some older browsers. Macromedia has a page that shows all the browsers that have a Flash plug-in available, at http://www.macromedia.com/support/shockwave/plug/brow. Another factor to consider is the browsers your audience will be using. One way to do this is to install a program to analyze the log files your Web server generates. If this is not a possibility for you, you can visit sites such as http://www.browserwatch.com to gather statistics about Web browser usage.

### Deciding Which Flash Version or File Type to Use

The Flash movie file type is .swf (Shockwave Flash). However, you can generate several other types of files. If you feel that your audience will largely consist of viewers with older browsers that will not support Flash files, you can export your movie as a Java applet. You can also export your movie as an AVI or an animated GIF, but these are not useful for our purposes, because AVIs and animated GIFs created from our movie would be incredibly large files. Furthermore, the AVI would not contain the link buttons. These would not be good choices for this particular page, but a Java applet may be a good choice. In addition to allowing you many file types for exporting movies, Flash even allows you to create a stand-alone projector, useful for kiosk or presentation applications. The next section will describe in detail how to create pages with some of these options.

## ◆ Publishing

Flash 4 provides a means to create Web pages easily with your Flash movie. Flash 4 can also convert the movie file into a Java applet, as well as creating the HTML code for the applet.

**NOTE**
You can download the project at this point from http://www.phptr.com/essential/flash/shelley/shelley3-6.html.

### Choosing Format Settings

Before you can use Flash to make your Web page, you will need to specify the settings for the Shelley Biotech Flash movie and associated files. First, you need to decide which formats you will support.

1. With the most recent version of the Shelley page open, choose the menu option File→Publish Settings.

2. The Publish Settings dialog box should appear (see Figure 4–4).

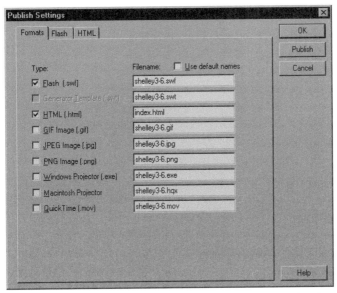

**FIGURE 4–4** Publish Settings dialog box with Formats tab selected

3. Click on the Formats tab.

4. Uncheck the Use Default Names box. This allows you to rename the automatically generated files.

5. Make sure the Flash and HTML boxes are checked, but none of the others.

6. Rename the file next to the HTML box "index.html."

7. The Flash program will generate an HTML page and the movie that will be embedded in it. These will be saved in the same directory as your .fla file. Leave the dialog box open for the next set of steps.

## Choosing Flash Settings

The Flash settings tab controls the way that Flash will process your movie.

1. The Publish Settings dialog box should be open. Choose the Flash tab (see Figure 4–5).

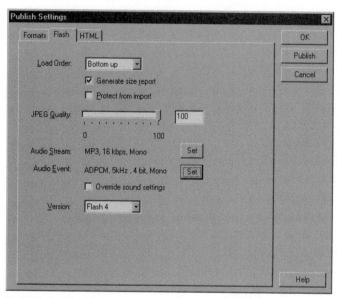

**FIGURE 4–5** Publish Settings dialog box with Flash tab selected

2. The Load Order should be Bottom Up. This controls the load order of the layers, so that the background layers will be loaded before the other layers.

3. Check the Generate Size Report button. A text file will be produced with file size information, useful for optimizing your movie. We will take a closer look at this report shortly.

4. Leave Protect From Import unchecked for the purposes of this book. Leaving this unclicked allows people to download your movie from your site.

5. Leave the JPEG quality set to 100. Any JPEGs on the page will be uncompressed. In our case, we have only the one small image, so this should not affect the final file size too much.

6. The Audio Stream settings are used to determine the quality and compression used for the streaming music on the site. Since we are not using any Audio Stream settings in this project, leave the setting as the default.

7. The Audio Event settings are used to determine the quality and compression used for the sound effects. Our buttons use sounds, so we should change this. Press the Set button and choose 5kHz for the rate and 4 bit ADPCM for the compression (see Figure 4–6). Click OK.

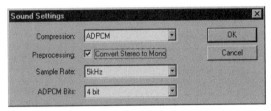

**FIGURE 4–6** Sound Settings dialog box

8. Set Version as Flash 4. The other options are Flash 1, Flash 2, and Flash 3, which are older versions of Flash. Although the Flash 4 plug-in supports these files, Flash 4 features will be disabled on movies exported as these types.

9. Do not close the dialog box. We will be making more changes momentarily.

## Choosing HTML Settings

The HTML Settings tab controls the formatting of the automatically produced HTML page.

1. The Publish Settings dialog box should be open. Choose the HTML tab (see Figure 4–7).

2. Flash offers a variety of different templates. Use the Info button to find out more about each one.

3. Choose the default template, Flash Only.

4. Dimensions should be Match Movie. This will display the movie at the actual size in which we created it. If you wish the movie to scale with the window, change to Percent and

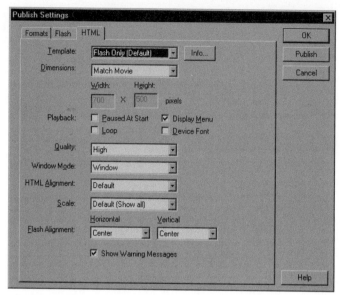

**FIGURE 4–7** Publish Settings dialog box with the HTML tab selected

specify 100 pixels x 100 pixels in the Width and Height boxes.

**5.** Make sure the Display Menu check box is selected. The other three Playback boxes should not be checked. The Display Menu option allows viewers to pull up a menu, as shown in Figure 4–8, using the right mouse button (PC) or Ctrl-click (Mac).

**FIGURE 4–8** Menu available to Flash viewers

6. Quality should be set to High.

7. Window Mode should be set to Window.

8. Leave both the HTML Alignment and Scale boxes set to Default.

9. Flash Alignment Horizontal and Vertical should both be set to Center.

10. Check the Show Warning Messages box.

## Publishing the Movie

You have two options for actually publishing the movie. You can click the Publish button located in the Publish Settings dialog box, or you can click OK in this dialog box and choose the menu option File→Publish. If you choose the second option, you can preview your page before actually publishing it by using the File→Publish Preview menu, and choose the HTML option.

## Viewing the Size Report

When we selected Publish settings, we instructed the program to create a size report. In the same directory as the .swf file is a file named shelley3-6 Report.txt. Let's take a look at each section.

| Frame # | Frame Bytes | Total Bytes | Page |
|---------|-------------|-------------|------|
| 1 | 28189 | 28189 | Scene 1 |
| 2 | 434 | 28623 | 2 |
| 3 | 424 | 29047 | 3 |
| 4 | 424 | 29471 | 4 |
| 5 | 431 | 29902 | 5 |
| 6 | 431 | 30333 | 6 |
| 7 | 429 | 30762 | 7 |
| 8 | 429 | 31191 | 8 |
| 9 | 428 | 31619 | 9 |
| 10 | 426 | 32045 | 10 |
| 11 | 426 | 32471 | 11 |
| 12 | 426 | 32897 | 12 |
| 13 | 431 | 33328 | 13 |
| 14 | 431 | 33759 | 14 |
| 15 | 361 | 34120 | 15 |
| 16 | 295 | 34415 | 16 |
| 17 | 295 | 34710 | 17 |
| 18 | 295 | 35005 | 18 |
| 19 | 295 | 35300 | 19 |

| | | | |
|---|---|---|---|
| 20 | 295 | 35595 | 20 |
| 21 | 295 | 35890 | 21 |
| 22 | 295 | 36185 | 22 |
| 23 | 295 | 36480 | 23 |
| 24 | 295 | 36775 | 24 |
| 25 | 295 | 37070 | 25 |
| 26 | 294 | 37364 | 26 |
| 27 | 292 | 37656 | 27 |
| 28 | 292 | 37948 | 28 |
| 29 | 292 | 38240 | 29 |
| 30 | 958 | 39198 | 30 |

Each of the frames of the animation is listed along with its size in bytes and a running total. It is important to notice that the first frame is by far the largest, and all of the following frames are tiny. This is due to the vector nature of the Flash format. The final file size is 39K. This is not incredibly large, but you'll see a way to shrink it substantially in a moment.

| Page | Shape Bytes | Text Bytes |
|---|---|---|
| Scene 1 | 97 | 122 |
| Embedded Objects | 57 | 0 |

The Page section contains only one scene, since there is only one scene in this movie. It breaks down the number of bytes used for shapes and texts.

| Symbol | Shape Bytes | Text Bytes |
|---|---|---|
| Address Text | 0 | 217 |
| Photo | 0 | 0 |
| Link Text | 0 | 333 |
| Lines | 54 | 0 |
| Brown Background | 48 | 0 |
| White Background | 48 | 0 |
| Link Circle | 349 | 0 |

Here's a list of the symbols and their bytes. All of these are quite small. This is not where most of the size is coming from.

| Bitmap | Compressed | Original | Compression |
|---|---|---|---|
| office.jpg | 22828 | 71920 | Imported JPEG |

Here's the problem! The photograph on our page adds nearly 23K. Notice that we left the Quality set at 100 when we saved this file.

```
Tweened Shapes: 411 bytes

Event sounds: 5KHz Mono 4 bit ADPCM

Sound Name          Bytes   Format
----------------    -----   ---------------------
Cloth Rip           408     5KHz Mono 4 bit ADPCM
```

The sound file we used takes up a bit of space also. There is not much we can do about this other than using the smallest possible sound files.

```
Font Name           Bytes   Characters
----------------    -----   -----------------------------------------
Arial Bold Italic   2727    !,.01ABCEHILMOSTVWYabcdefhilmnoprstuvwy
```

This is a list of the text characters used on our page. Nearly 3K may seem a bit large, until you consider that letters can be reused without adding to this size. As long as you use the same font on the page, you can have as much text as you like without greatly increasing the size of the movie.

## *Optimizing the Movie*

After looking over the size report, we find that the only major problem is that the office photo must be uncompressed.

1.  Choose Window→Library.

2.  Locate the office photo. Be careful not to select the symbol we named "Photo," but rather the JPEG image from which it was created.

3.  Choose Properties from the Options menu (see Figure 4–9).

4.  Change the JPEG Quality to 30. Leave the other settings as before. Click OK.

Now let's glance at the size report again. The size is now 19K! This is much better. Specifically, the photo is now around 3K in size. This will tremendously reduce download time. If you can get by with few to no raster graphics, your movie will be much more compact. It's time to publish our movie.

While Flash is an extremely robust application offering you many options for producing your movie, there may be times when you do not want to use it to create the HTML. Perhaps you don't have it available, or you simply wish to gain an understanding of

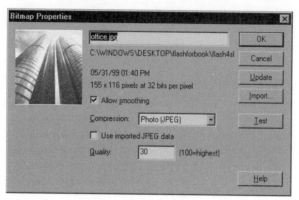

**FIGURE 4-9** Bitmap Properties dialog box

the HTML code necessary to play your movie. This section offers you some insight on the HTML side of things. You are assumed to have a basic knowledge of HTML tags. Tags that are not specifically discussed are common HTML tags that you can look up in an HTML reference.

## Writing the HTML for the .swf File

When you saved your movie from the Flash 4 program, you named it shelley3-6.swf. To generate only a movie and no HTML files, you need to uncheck the HTML box on the Formats tab of the Publish Settings dialog box. The code you would need to publish this to an HTML file follows, along with a discussion of the various tags specific to the Flash files.

```
<HTML>
<HEAD>
<TITLE>Shelley Biotech</TITLE>
</HEAD>
<BODY bgcolor="#CCCC99">
```

This bgcolor matches our movie. You will need to add the text and link colors you want unless the browser defaults are sufficient.

```
<OBJECT classid=
 "clsid:D27CDB6E-AE6D-11cf-96B8-444553540000"
 ID=shelley WIDTH=100% HEIGHT=100%>
```

The OBJECT tag is used for Internet Explorer to allow the Flash to be embedded as an Active X control. This is only necessary if you wish to allow your Flash movie to be viewable on an IE browser with a Flash Active X control. The `classid` value identifies the specific Active X control to use. The `WIDTH` and `HEIGHT` tags are responsible for making the Active X control match the browser size. This can be hardwired as a specific pixel size by removing the % sign and changing these values.

```
<PARAM NAME=movie VALUE="shelley3-6.swf">
```

The `PARAM` tags tell the Flash player how the movie should be displayed. This first one points at the .swf file to use.

```
<PARAM NAME=loop VALUE=false>
```

This `PARAM` tag tells the Flash player to play this file a single time and then to stop. If you wished the file to loop indefinitely, you would set this to `true`.

```
<PARAM NAME=quality VALUE=high>
```

The quality `PARAM` tag tells the Flash player to display this movie with the highest possible image quality.

```
<PARAM NAME=bgcolor VALUE=#CCCC99>
```

The background color of the Flash player area should match the page background and the movie background.

```
<EMBED SRC="shelley3-6.swf" WIDTH=100% HEIGHT=100%
LOOP=false
QUALITY=high
BGCOLOR=#CCCC99
TYPE="application/x-shockwave-flash" >
```

The `EMBED` tag is used to call the Flash player and tell it how to play the movie.

```
</EMBED>
</OBJECT>
</BODY>
</HTML>
```

## Creating a Non-Flash Version of the Page

Flash provides a means for creating static pages from your Flash movie. Flash can create a static GIF with an image map from one of the frames from your Flash movie.

1. Select the frame in your movie of which you wish to create a static GIF. In the case of the Shelley site, it should be the last frame, frame 30.

2. Double-click on the 30th frame. This opens the Frame Properties dialog box.

3. Click on the Label tab and enter "#Static" in the blank. Choose the Label radio button (see Figure 4–10). Click OK.

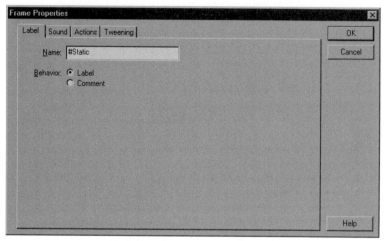

**FIGURE 4–10** Frame Properties dialog box with Label tab selected

4. With the current version of the Shelley page, choose File→Publish Settings.

5. Select the Formats tab. Check the box next to GIF Image (see Figure 4–11).

6. Now select the HTML tab. If you wish to create both a Flash version and an image map version, choose the Template setting Flash 4 with Image, as shown in Figure 4–12. If you want to create only an image map so that you can see what it will look like to browsers without Flash, choose Image Map from the Template list box.

7. Finally, choose the GIF tab and use the settings shown in Figure 4–13.

8. Click Publish and then click OK. Use File→Publish Preview to view the various files that Flash will create with the chosen

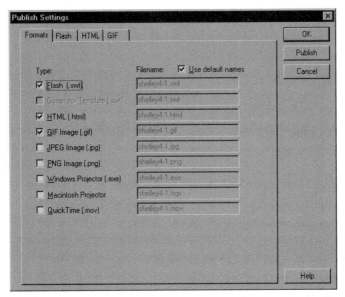

**FIGURE 4–11** Publish Settings dialog box with Formats tab selected

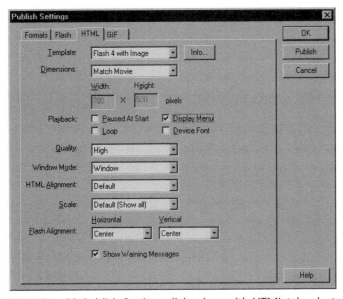

**FIGURE 4–12** Publish Settings dialog box with HTML tab selected

settings. Keep in mind that GIF images have palettes limited to 256 colors or less, so any photos or gradient fills on your page will not look very good.

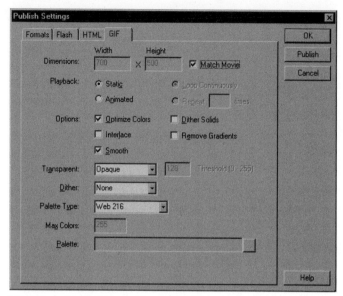

**FIGURE 4–13** Publish Settings dialog box with GIF tab selected

## A Few Final Web Publishing Issues

If you use Flash to create your HTML file, you may have to hand-edit the HTML file produced, should you FTP or otherwise move this file. Flash may put hard paths to files in the code that will need to be changed to reflect the move. Also make sure that the appropriate Java files reside in the specified directory for any Java applets you produce and move. Finally, Flash may produce more than an HTML file, so make sure you move the .htm, .swf, and all other files associated with your page to the appropriate directory. An example of this is when you tell Flash to produce a static GIF file for browsers with no Flash support. Flash creates a .gif file as well as the .html.

**NOTE**

This would be a good time to save your work or download the project at this point from http://www.phptr.com/essential/flash/shelley/shelley4-1.html.

# ◆ Preloading

Preloading is a technique used to let the viewer know the page is being loaded. Instead of viewers being presented with a blank page, a graphic can be used to indicate that loading is taking place. This section will explain how to add a simple preload scene to the Shelley page.

**NOTE**
You can download this project at this point from http://www.phptr.com/essential/flash/shelley/shelley4-1.html.

## *Adding a Scene to the Current Movie*

1.  Open the current shelley.fla or download and open shelley4-1.fla.

2.  Choose Insert→Scene. You are now presented with a new blank scene. To change the current scene, use the Scene List button, shown just above frame 24 in Figure 4–14.

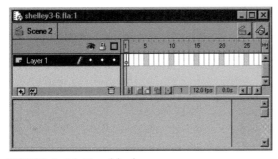

**FIGURE 4–14** New blank scene

3.  Open the Scene Inspector, shown in Figure 4–15, by choosing Window→Inspectors→Scene.

4.  Highlight Scene 1 in this dialog box and choose Properties. Scene 1 is the scene with the graphics and animation.

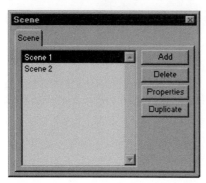

**FIGURE 4–15** Scene Inspector dialog box

> **5.** Change its name to "Main" and click OK (see Figure 4–16).

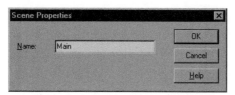

**FIGURE 4–16** Scene Properties dialog box

> **6.** Highlight Scene 2 in this dialog box and choose Properties. Scene 2 is the scene we just added.
>
> **7.** Change its name to "Preload" and click OK.
>
> **8.** Finally, the order of the scenes needs to be changed. Click and drag the Preload label above the Main label, as shown in Figure 4–17. Now the Preload scene will play, followed by the Main scene.

### Modifying the Preload Scene

> **1.** Make sure the currently selected scene is the Preload scene.
>
> **2.** Choose Insert Layer. This scene now has two layers.
>
> **3.** Rename the top layer "Tags."
>
> **4.** Rename the bottom layer "Actions."
>
> **5.** Click on keyframe 1 in the Tags layer. Choose Modify→ Frame.

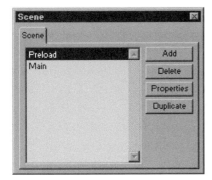

**FIGURE 4–17** Scene Inspector dialog box

    **6.** Select the Label tab (see Figure 4–18).

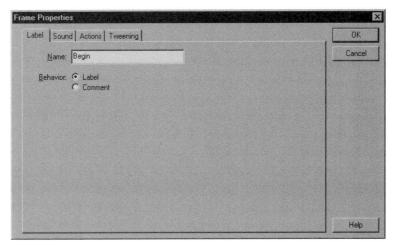

**FIGURE 4–18** Frame Properties dialog box

    **7.** Type "Begin" for the label name. The Behavior should be set to Label. Click OK.

## Creating the Preloading Animation

    **1.** Click on keyframe 1 of the Actions layer.

    **2.** Select the Text tool and type the words "Page Loading," using Arial for the font, black for the color, and 48 for the size.

3. Move the text with the Arrow to the center of the scene. You may want to use the Modify→Align option to center it (see Figure 4–19).

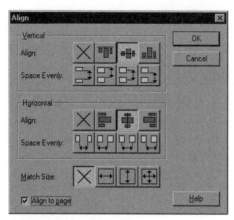

**FIGURE 4–19** Align dialog box

4. Select this text and choose Insert→Convert to Symbol.

5. Name this symbol "Loading" and choose Graphic for Behavior. Click OK.

6. Insert a keyframe at frame 10 for both the Tags and Actions layers.

7. Click on keyframe 10 of the Actions layer. We will make the loading text fade out.

8. Select the loading text and choose Modify→Instance.

9. Click on the Color Effect tab in the Instance Properties dialog box (see Figure 4–20).

10. Choose Alpha from the list box and move the slider to 0%. Click OK.

11. To add Tweening, select the first keyframe of the Actions layer and choose Modify→Frame.

12. Select the Tweening tab and choose Motion (see Figure 4–21). Click OK.

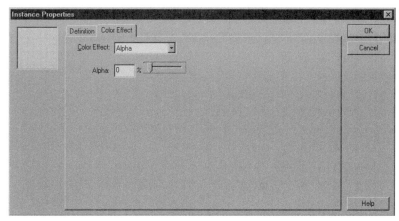

**FIGURE 4–20** Instance Properties dialog box

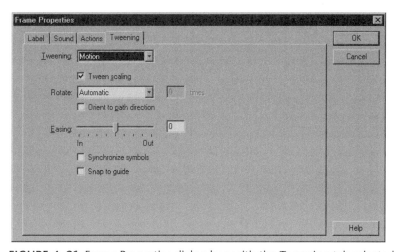

**FIGURE 4–21** Frame Properties dialog box with the Tweening tab selected

## Adding the Action Code

The only thing left to do is to add the code to tell the preloader when to quit playing.

1. Select the first keyframe in the Actions layer of the Pre-load scene.

2. Choose Modify→Frame.

3. Select the Actions tab.

**4.** Click on the Plus sign and select If Frame Is Loaded from the menu (see Figure 4–22).

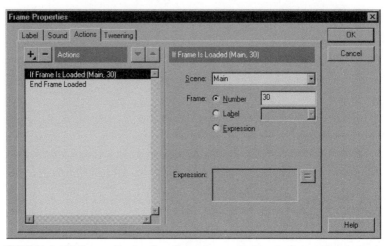

**FIGURE 4–22** Frame Properties dialog box with the Actions tab selected

**5.** On the right side of the Actions tab, choose Main from the Scene list box.

**6.** Select Number for the Frame option, and enter 30.

**7.** Now click on the Plus sign again to add another action. Choose Go To and Play (see Figure 4–23).

**8.** On the right side of the Actions tab, choose Main for the Scene.

**9.** Select Number for Frame and enter 1.

**10.** Make sure the Go To and Play check box is selected. Click OK.

**11.** Click on the keyframe at frame 10 of the Actions layer. Choose Modify→Frame.

**12.** Select the Actions tab.

**13.** Choose Go To and Play from the Plus menu (see Figure 4–24).

**14.** For the Scene option on the right, choose Preload.

**15.** Select the Label option for Frame and choose Begin from the list box.

**16.** Make sure the Go To and Play check box is selected. Click OK.

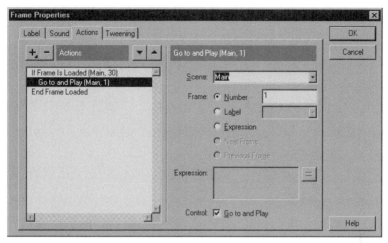

**FIGURE 4–23** Frame Properties dialog box with the Actions tab selected

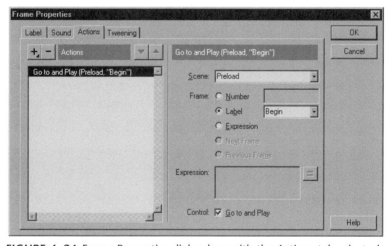

**FIGURE 4–24** Frame Properties dialog box with the Actions tab selected

## Putting in a Stop Action

The last thing we need to do is add a Stop action to the Main scene. Without this in place, the movie will loop.

1. Use the Scene list button to change to the Main scene.

2. Select the final keyframe of any layer. The example file uses the Header Text layer.

**3.** Choose Modify→Frame. Select the Actions tab.

**4.** Click on the Plus menu and choose Stop. Click OK.

That's it. You now have a very simple preloader that will play the loading animation until the final frame of the movie is loaded. To preview your movie, choose Control→Test Movie. You will probably not see the preloader scene using this, as all the graphics are already in memory and quickly accessed. You can also use the File→Publish Preview option to test it out, and the File→Publish option to create a final version. You may need to actually upload your HTML and .swf files to a Web server to slow down the loading enough for the preloader to be noticeable.

## ◆ Detecting the Plug-In

Several techniques are used to manage detection of the Flash Plug-in. The simplest involve self-selection; the most complex use scripting languages. This section will discuss the reasoning behind using one over another and will provide you with a scheme for using Flash to accomplish plug-in detection.

The simplest technique is to allow the user to self-select. In this scenario, the user is presented with a basic HTML page with a link for both a Flash version and a non-Flash version of the site. This assumes that users know whether or not they have the plug-in. Many average users probably do not know, so this is not necessarily the best choice.

Building on the idea of self-selection, the users may again be presented with a choice, but this time a small Flash movie can be embedded in the page. The page should point out to the users that they should enter the Flash site if they can see the animation in the movie. In both cases it's a good idea to put in links to Macromedia's site and to give instructions on getting the plug-in. Flash has a template under the Publish Settings menu that does this for you. You may have to hand-edit the page to add the appropriate text for your particular page.

Using JavaScript to detect the plug-in has definite advantages. The user does not have to make any choices and can be automatically pointed to the appropriate page. The main disadvantage to using JavaScript is that the scripts tend to be long and complicated. If you decide to use it, you should search on the Web for scripts already written for this purpose. A good place to look is http://www.FlashCentral.com/Tech/Detect/.

The best middle-of-the-road approach to detecting the plug-in is to use Flash. Since Flash supports frame actions, a small movie on a page can be directed to load another page when it hits a specific frame. Only browsers with the plug-in installed will be able to execute the command.

### Modifying the Movie for Flash Detection

1. Choose File→New.

2. Open the Movie Properties dialog box by choosing Modify→ Movie.

3. Change the movie to the smallest allowable size, 18 pixels x 18 pixels (see Figure 4–25).

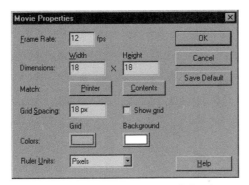

**FIGURE 4–25** Movie Properties dialog box

4. Change the background color to match your page. This is the light tan color in the fifth column and third row from the bottom (see Figure 4–26). Click OK.

5. Choose the Layer 1 keyframe at frame 1.

6. Select Modify→Frame.

7. Select the Actions tab (see Figure 4–27).

8. Choose Get URL from the Plus menu and enter the appropriate URL on the right. This will be the location of the Flash version of the site.

9. Choose _self from the Window list box. If you want to load the Flash site in another window, use _blank. Click OK.

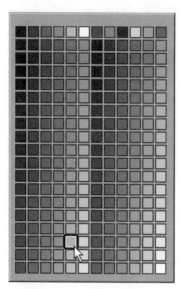

**FIGURE 4–26** Color palette

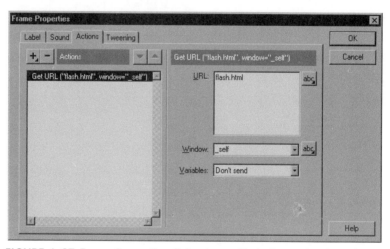

**FIGURE 4–27** Frame Properties dialog box with Actions tab selected

10. Choose File→Publish Settings. Under the Formats tab, only the Flash check box should be selected (see Figure 4–28).

11. Uncheck the Use default names box and type the name "detect.swf" next to the Flash check box.

12. Click Publish and click OK.

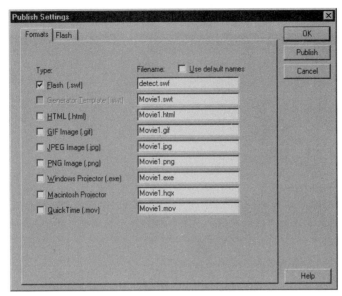

**FIGURE 4-28** Publish Settings dialog box with Formats tab selected

## *Creating the HTML Page for This Movie*

The movie we just created needs to be embedded in an HTML page. The source code that follows demonstrates a page that sends browsers without the plug-in to another page after several seconds.

```
<HTML>
<HEAD>
<TITLE>Shelley Biotech Flash Site</TITLE>

<!-The Meta statement below automatically redirects non-flash enabled
browsers to index2.html, a static version of the Shelley page. --!>

<META HTTP-EQUIV="Refresh" CONTENT="15; URL=index2.html">
</HEAD>

<BODY BGCOLOR="# CCCC99">

<OBJECT CLASSID="clsid:D27CDB6E-AE6D-11cf-96B8-444553540000"
WIDTH=" HEIGHT=" CODEBASE="http://active.macromedia.com/flash3/cabs/">
    <PARAM NAME="MOVIE" VALUE="flash2check.swf">
    <PARAM NAME="PLAY" VALUE="true">
    <PARAM NAME="LOOP" VALUE="false">
    <PARAM NAME="QUALITY" VALUE="high">
```

```
<PARAM NAME="SCALE" VALUE="SHOWALL">
    <EMBED SRC="shelley.swf" WIDTH="18" HEIGHT="18" PLAY="true"
    LOOP="false" QUALITY="high" SCALE="SHOWALL"
    PLUGINSPAGE="http://www.macromedia.com/shockwave/download
    /index.cgi?P1_Prod_Version=ShockwaveFlash">
    </EMBED>
</OBJECT>
</BODY>
</HTML>
```

# ◆ Web Server Settings

Before a Flash movie can be viewed on the Web, the Web server must know how to deliver it. Web servers have configuration files with a list of Multipurpose Internet Mail Extensions (MIME) types. When a Web server receives a request for a file with a listed MIME type, it sends a file descriptor, followed by the requested file. The browser then knows which plug-in to use to display the file. If the Web server is correctly configured, you will be able to upload your files into your Web directory and be able to view them correctly in a browser with the correct Flash plug-in. If you can't view the file, or the Web server sends you a text page, you should contact your Internet Service Provider's system administrator or technical support person and ask that the Web server's MIME types be modified to send Flash 4 correctly. If you manage your own Web server, brief instructions for modifying some of the more popular Web servers follow.

## Configuring Apache

1. Locate the mime.types file in your Apache conf/ directory.

2. Edit this file and add the line:

```
application/x-shockwave-flash    swf
```

3. Save the file and restart the Apache server.

## Configuring IIS 4.0

1. Choose from the Start menu Programs→Windows NT 4.0 Option Pack→Microsoft Internet Information Server→ Internet Service Manager.

2. From the Console dialog box, select Console Root→Internet Information Server→Your Computer.

3. Right-click on Your Computer.

4. Choose Properties from the menu.

5. Click the File Types button.

6. In the File Type dialog box, type `.swf` as an Associated Extension.

7. For Content Type, type `application/x-shockwave-flash`.

8. Click OK on all the dialog boxes.

For other Web servers, view the help documents for instructions on inserting MIME types. The specific information needed by all servers is

```
MIME Type:  application/x-shockwave-flash    Suffix:  .swf
```

In this chapter we have finished the Shelley Biotech homepage by publishing it to the Web. This project touched on many of the basic features of Flash. The second half of this book will focus on building a more elaborate Flash project, with a greater emphasis on interactivity and multimedia.

## RECAP

In this chapter you learned how to:
- Publish a Flash movie to the Web in different formats
- Preload a Flash movie
- Detect the Flash Plug-In
- Set up a Web server for Flash

## ADVANCED PROJECTS

1. Change the static GIF Flash produces to a different frame.

2. Try publishing the Shelley page with different Template options from the HTML tab of the Publish Settings dialog box and test the results on different browsers.

3. Change the browser detection method.

# 5 Fine-Tuning Graphics

## IN THIS CHAPTER

* Reshaping
* Intersections
* Brush Effects
* Recap
* Advanced Projects

*The next three chapters will be devoted to developing the* Stitch *site. Stitch is an online fashion magazine with some bells and whistles the Shelley Biotech site did not have. The* Stitch *site has an animated splash screen, a Flash-based menuing system, a contact form, and an interactive fashion show. In this chapter you will learn some more advanced graphic techniques, including modification of basic shapes and intersections. The* Stitch *Web site splash screen will be created.*

## ◆ Reshaping

Drawing shapes freehand to achieve the effect you desire can be very difficult. It is often easier to draw a rough approximation of the desired shape and then manipulate it into the final image. Flash provides a very simple way to modify shapes and lines.

So far, you have used the Arrow tool to select, resize, rotate, and move graphic objects. It is also used to reshape graphics. To try it out, open Flash and draw something. Switch to the Arrow tool. Do not click on the graphic, but instead move the cursor to the edge of the graphic. The cursor will change to look like one of the two cursors shown in Figure 5–1. At this point, if you click, hold, and drag the edge of your graphic, you will reshape it. The curve under the arrow means that you will be moving a curve, the angle means that you are at a corner or endpoint. In this section, you will be creating and reshaping graphics for the splash screen.

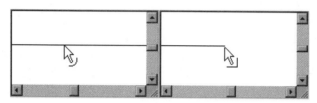

**FIGURE 5–1** Adding curves to lines and moving endpoints of lines

For the splash screen, we will be using a dark blue background with white and gray graphics and text. A preview of the splash screen is shown in Figure 5–2.

### Getting Started

1.  Start the Flash program. A new blank movie should appear.

2.  Choose Modify→Movie.

3.  Change the background color to the dark blue in the first column of the third row (see Figure 5–3).

4.  Change the size of the movie to 600 pixels x 500 pixels.

5.  Set the frame rate to 12 fps.

6.  Change the grid spacing to 10 pixels. Select OK.

**NOTE**
This would be a good time to save your work. Choose File→Save As, and save this file as stitch.fla in the directory of your choice. Download the project at this point from http://www.phptr.com/essential/ flash/stitch/stitch5-1.html.

**FIGURE 5–2** Splash screen. (Image ©1999 MJ Wilson.)

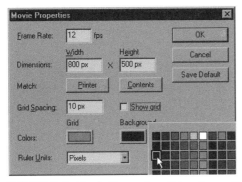

**FIGURE 5–3** Movie Properties dialog box with the background color palette

## Drawing the Needle Graphic

Looking back at Figure 5–2, you will notice a sewing needle graphic. The steps that follow describe how to draw the outline of the needle, as seen in Figure 5–4.

1. Begin by making the grid visible by choosing View→Grid.

2. Select the View→Snap option.

**FIGURE 5–4** Outline of needle

3. You may want to change the grid color to a darker one to see the image you will be creating more clearly. Select Modify→Movie and change the grid color to a dark gray.

4. Change to the Oval tool. The line color should be white, thickness should be 1.0, and the style should be solid. Make the fill transparent (see Figure 5–5).

**FIGURE 5–5** Oval tool settings

5. Open the Object Inspector window.

6. Draw an oval.

7. Select the oval you just created and use the Object Inspector to change it to approximately 300 pixels in height and 40 pixels in width.

8. Change to the Arrow tool. Deselect the oval.

9. We are now going to change the shape of this oval to the needle outline. You will be moving the outline. Move your arrow over the oval outline on the left side near the center, as shown in Figure 5-6. With the arrow cursor changed to look like the one in the image, hold down the mouse button and drag the outline toward the center of the oval until it resembles the figure. Do the same thing for the right side.

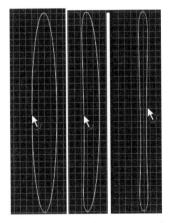

FIGURE 5–6 Reshape the oval

10. Next, we need to make the point of the needle. On the outline at approximately 20 pixels from the bottom of the oval, click, hold, and drag the outline toward the center line on each side, as shown in Figure 5–7.

11. The last step is to add the eye of the needle. Select the Oval tool. The options should still be the same as those you used for drawing the needle outline.

12. Turn off Snap to grid.

13. Near the upper part of the needle, draw a tall thin circle for the eye. If you need to adjust this circle, change to the Arrow tool and click on it to select it. You can then move it or reshape it as necessary.

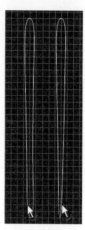

**FIGURE 5–7** Create the point of the needle

**NOTE**

This would be a good time to save your work or download the project at this point from http://www.phptr.com/essential/flash/ stitch/stitch5-2.html.

## Filling in Needle Texture

Now that you have drawn the needle outline, it's time to fill it with a texture.

1. Choose the Paint Bucket.

2. Click on the Fill Color button.

3. Click on the button in the top center of the color sub-menu. This will open the Color dialog box so you can create a new texture (see Figure 5–8).

4. Click on the Gradient tab of the Color dialog box (see Figure 5–9).

5. Create a gradient with two colors. The color on the left should have RGB values of 200, 200, 200. The color on the right should be 45, 45, 45. Change the type in the drop-down list to Linear.

6. Click on the New button and close the Color dialog box. The texture should now be selected.

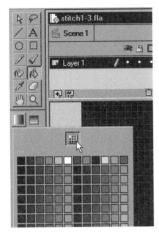

**FIGURE 5–8** Click button on Color palette to open Color dialog box

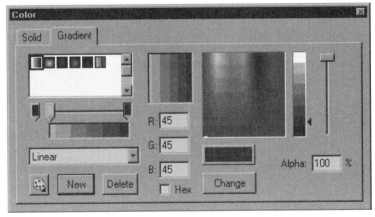

**FIGURE 5–9** Color dialog box with Gradient tab selected

7. Use the Paint Bucket and click inside the needle outline to fill it.

8. Change to the Arrow tool. Select the white outlines and delete them.

## Tilting the Needle

We need to rotate the needle to a more pleasing angle.

1. Change to the Arrow.

2. Select the needle.

3. Click on the Rotate option near the bottom of the Tool palette.

4. Click, hold, and move one of the corner handles until the needle angle resembles Figure 5–10.

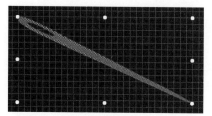

**FIGURE 5–10** Tilted needle

**NOTE**

This would be a good time to save your work or download the project at this point from http://www.phptr.com/essential/flash/stitch/stitch5-3.html.

## Drawing the Thread

Now we will draw the thread that hangs from the needle.

1. You will need a new layer for the thread. Choose the Insert Layer option from the Layer menu. Name the new layer "Thread." You should also change the name of Layer 1 to "Needle."

2. Hide the grid by unchecking View→Grid.

3. Make sure the Thread layer is currently selected. Choose the Pencil tool.

4. The Pencil settings should be changed, as seen in Figure 5–11. The Pencil Mode should be Smooth, the color White, a thickness of 2.0, and the style should be dashed.

5. Draw two wavy lines from the eye of the needle to resemble those in Figure 5–12. You do not have to draw them exactly as you want them to look. You can change to the Arrow tool and reshape them. It is very easy to modify and lengthen the lines with the Arrow tool.

**FIGURE 5–11** Pencil settings

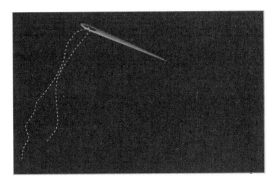

**FIGURE 5–12** Needle with thread

6. Move the needle and thread lines approximately to the locations shown in Figure 5–12.

## ◆ Intersections

In addition to reshaping, Flash offers another useful feature for creating custom images: A graphic can be subtracted from another graphic. Basically, this means that you can create images with holes in them. This is accomplished by creating two graphics in the same layer, dragging one on top of the other, and then deleting the top one. For example, if you want to make a doughnut shape, you can create two filled circles, one much larger than the other, and then move the smaller one to the center of the large one and deselect both. Finally, select the small circle and delete it, and you are left with a large filled circle with a hole in it. As soon as the top one is deselected, it erases anything that was underneath it. It can then be moved or deleted, and empty space remains. Also, if the top graphic went all the way across the bottom one, the bottom one is now in two separate pieces. Figure 5–13 should make this more clear.

**FIGURE 5–13** Intersecting two shapes

This image shows two objects and the results of deleting the top one, and also the components that result from their intersection.

Next you will use intersection to create the button image, create the *Stitch* text, and add the image.

### Creating the Button Texture

The button texture consists of a gradient fill with three colors. Figure 5–14 shows the Color dialog box with the gradient. To create this texture:

1. Select the Paint Bucket.

2. Click on the Color button, then on the Color Edit button at the top of the palette.

3. Click on the Gradient tab.

4. Set the style in the drop-down box to Radial.

5. You now should see two color markers. Notice the color marker to the left of the others. This is used to add more colors to the gradient. Drag an additional color marker to

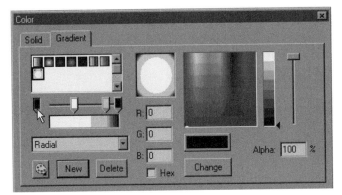

**FIGURE 5–14** Color dialog box with Gradient tab selected

the right by clicking and holding on the color marker on the left, shown in Figure 5–14 next to the mouse pointer. Click and drag the three markers in the same approximate locations as shown in the diagram.

6. Click on each color marker to change the colors. The RGB values of the three, from left to right, are 255, 255, 255 (white), 193, 193, 193 (gray), and 0, 0, 51 (dark blue).

7. Click New and close the Color dialog box.

8. Create a new layer by choosing Insert→Layer. Name it "Button."

9. Select the Button layer and hide the others with the Layer menu.

10. Use the Oval tool with the options shown in Figure 5–15. The Line Color should be transparent, Line Thickness should be 1.0, Line Style should be Solid, and the Fill Color should be the new one we just created.

11. Draw a circle of any size. Use the Object Inspector to change it to a 70 height by 70 width pixel circle (see Figure 5–16).

**NOTE**
This would be a good time to save your work or download the project at this point from http://www.phptr.com/essential/flash/stitch/stitch5-4.html.

**FIGURE 5–15** Oval tool and settings

**FIGURE 5–16** Circle with new fill

## Creating the Buttonholes

We will now use intersection to create the buttonholes, then add small objects to give the illusion of thread. Figure 5–17 shows the button and the approximate size of the buttonholes you need to create.

**FIGURE 5–17** Buttonholes and button

1.  Select Button as the current layer.

2.  Change to the Oval tool. Select a light gray color and the settings shown in Figure 5–18.

**FIGURE 5–18** Oval tool and settings

3.  Draw a small oval, as shown in the figure.

4.  Select the oval and choose Edit→Copy.

5.  Choose Edit→Paste to place a new copy of the oval.

6.  Select and move the copy next to the original, as shown. It may be helpful to select both images and use the Modify→ Align dialog box.

7.  Select both ovals and place them in the center of the button. Do not deselect them until you have placed them exactly where they need to go.

8.  To create the intersection, simply deselect all by clicking on a blank part of the work area. Move the button to the side. It will now have the buttonholes in it.

9.  Select and delete the two ovals.

**NOTE**

This would be a good time to save your work or download the project at this point from http://www.phptr.com/essential/flash/ stitch/stitch5-5.html.

## Adding the Thread Fill to the Buttonholes

1. To add the thread illusion, you will need a new texture. Choose the Paint Bucket, click on the Color button, and then open the Color dialog box by clicking on the bottom button.

2. Choose the Gradient tab. Click on one of the saved textures with a sphere shape (see Figure 5–19).

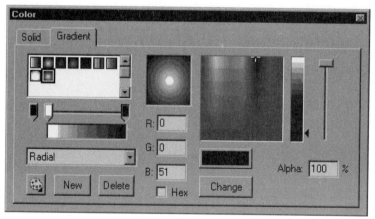

**FIGURE 5–19** Color dialog box with Gradient tab selected

3. The new gradient fill should go from white (255, 255, 255) to the same dark blue as the background (0, 0, 51).

4. Select New and close the Color dialog box.

5. Change to the Paint Bucket tool. Click in the center of each of the buttonholes to fill with this texture.

6. Your button should now look like Figure 5–20.

7. Select the button and buttonholes and choose Modify→ Group.

**FIGURE 5–20** Button with filled buttonholes

**NOTE**
This would be a good time to save your work or download the project at this point from http://www.phptr.com/essential/flash/stitch/stitch5-6.html.

Now that you have created the needle, thread, and button, you should add the main title text and begin placing objects on the page. The font used in the *Stitch* example is Mona Lisa Solid, but many other fonts could be used in its place. It was chosen because of its very bold quality.

## Creating the Text

The text on the splash screen consists of the title, the subtitle, and the article teaser.

1. Choose View→Antialias Text.

2. Create a new layer and name it "Text." Right-click (PC) or Ctrl-click (Mac) on this layer to open the Layer menu and hide the others.

3. Select the Text tool. Choose Mona Lisa Solid or something similar for the font, white for the color, and 48 for the size.

4. Click on the scene and add the text "Stitch." At this point the size does not matter; we can resize it later if necessary. Deselect the text (see Figure 5–21).

5. Change to a font size of 28. Click on a different area of the screen and type the text as shown in Figure 5–22: "In this month's issue, Stitch has got the Blues." Put a carriage return after the comma. Deselect the text.

6. Highlight just the word "Blues" with the text cursor (see Figure 5–23).

**FIGURE 5–21** Stitch text created

**FIGURE 5–22** Blues text added

**FIGURE 5–23** Blues text with the word "Blues" highlighted

7. Click on the Color palette and select a light blue color. The example site is using RGB 51, 153, 204. Click somewhere else on the scene.

8. Change the font size to 48 and the color to medium gray.

9. Type the text "Fashion Journal" (see Figure 5–24).

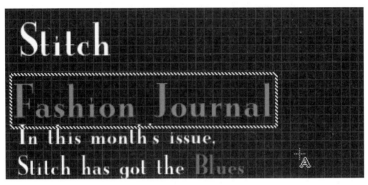

**FIGURE 5–24** "Fashion Journal" text added

10. Change to the Arrow. Click on the "Stitch" text and open the Object Inspector.

11. Resize the text to approximately 500 pixels wide by 90 pixels high, as shown in Figure 5–25.

**FIGURE 5–25** Resized "Stitch" text

12. Choose Show All from the Layer menu.

13. The other two text objects do not need to be resized. Move all the graphics to the appropriate locations, as seen in Figure 5–26.

14. Select the threads and the needle and choose Modify→ Group to group them together.

**FIGURE 5–26** Graphics moved to final locations

**NOTE**
This would be a good time to save your work or download the project at this point from http://www.phptr.com/essential/flash/ stitch/stitch5-7.html.

## Coloring the Text

To add a little more visual interest to the "Stitch" text, we will add the same gradient fill as was used for the button graphic. Since text objects can't be given gradient fills, we will convert it to a nontext graphic. The text before and after the fill is applied is shown in Figure 5–27. The difference is subtle.

**FIGURE 5–27** Unfilled and filled "Stitch"

1. Turn off the grid if it is on. Hide all layers except the Text layer.
2. Select the "Stitch" text. Make sure nothing else is currently selected.

3. Choose the menu option Modify→Break Apart.

4. Deselect the text.

5. Change to the Paint Bucket. Select the gradient you used for the button fill.

6. Click on the center area of each letter to apply the fill. You will have to treat the dot above the letter "i" as a separate object.

7. Change to the Arrow tool and, holding down the Shift key, select all the pieces. Choose Modify→Group. This will group the text. Choose Show All from the Layer menu.

**NOTE**
This would be a good time to save your work or download the project at this point from http://www.phptr.com/essential/flash/ stitch/stitch5-8.html.

## Adding the Photographic Image

The photo used on this page was edited in a different graphics program so that it would have the same background color as the page.

1. This image can be downloaded from the Web at http:// www.phptr.com/essential/flash/stitch/misc/splash.jpg.

2. Create and select a new layer called "Photo."

3. Select File→Import and select the image from wherever you saved it.

4. Use the Arrow to select and move the image to its appropriate location (see Figure 5–28).

5. Change the layer order to: Button, Thread, Text, Needle, Photo.

**NOTE**
This would be a good time to save your work or download the project at this point from http://www.phptr.com/essential/flash/ stitch/stitch5-9.html.

**FIGURE 5–28** Photograph imported and moved. (Image ©1999 MJ Wilson.)

## ◆ Brush Effects

The Brush tool is very powerful for creating freehand graphics. On this splash page it is used for the free-form shadows from the photo and the button.

### Creating the Shadow for the Button and Photo

1. Create a new layer and call it "Shadows." Make sure it is selected.

2. Click and drag the Shadows layer above the Photo layer if it is not already there.

3. Change to the Brush tool.

4. Choose Paint Normal for the Brush Mode. Choose the fifth brush size in the list, shown in Figure 5–29.

5. Use the round brush shape. Use black for the Fill Color (see Figure 5–30).

6. Make sure you are in the Shadows layer.

7. Draw a shadow shape next to the button.

8. Draw shadow shape next to the photo. Figures 5–31 and 5–32 show the shadows against a white movie background

**FIGURE 5–29** The brush size list

**FIGURE 5–30** Brush tool with settings

so you can see the shapes more clearly. The edges will be softened later.

**FIGURE 5–31** Model photograph with shadow. (Image ©1999 MJ Wilson.)

**FIGURE 5–32** Button with shadow

**NOTE**
This would be a good time to save your work or download the project at this point from http://www.phptr.com/essential/flash/ stitch/stitch5-10.html.

The shadow may be too long, or it may have edges that should be smoothed. Brush shapes can be treated just like any other shapes in Flash. To modify the size, select the shadow and use the Scale and Rotate button to make the desired changes. To change the edges, deselect the shadow. Move the mouse cursor to the edge that you wish to modify. When the cursor changes, click and drag the edge to modify it.

### Creating Gradient for Shadows

We should give the shadows a softer edge. We can do this by creating a gradient that changes from black at the center to transparent at the edge.

1. Click on the Paint Bucket.

2. Open the Color dialog box to create a new gradient fill.

3. As you can see in Figure 5–33, the type is Radial. It should have two colors near each other, as shown. In the example

both are black. The difference between them is that the one on the right has an Alpha value of zero, making it transparent.

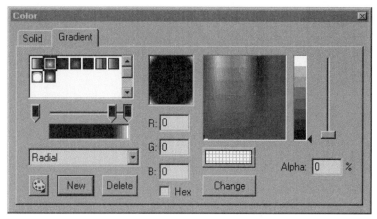

FIGURE 5–33 Color dialog box with Gradient tab selected

4. Click New and close the Color dialog box.

5. Click near the center of each of the two shadows to fill with the new texture. Notice that only the right and left edges are soft. We still need to modify the fill.

**NOTE**
This would be a good time to save your work or download the project at this point from http://www.phptr.com/essential/flash/stitch/stitch5-11.html.

## Modifying the Shadow Gradient

1. You will be using the Paint Bucket. Select the Transform Fill button, shown just above the mouse cursor in Figure 5–34.

2. Click on the large shadow. A circle indicating the gradient size and orientation will appear (see Figure 5–35).

3. Notice the three handles on the right side of the circle. The first one, the square, is used to resize the circle. Click,

**FIGURE 5–34** Paint Bucket tool

**FIGURE 5–35** Large shadow with Transform Fill circle. (Image ©1999 MJ Wilson.)

hold, and move the circle toward the center until the circle looks like Figure 5–36.

**FIGURE 5–36** Transform Fill circle with shape changed

4. The second handle is used to control the size of the circle. For the moment, leave it the same.

5. The third handle controls the rotation. Rotate it to resemble Figure 5–37.

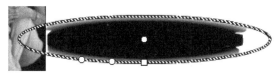

**FIGURE 5–37** Transform Fill circle rotated. (Image ©1999 MJ Wilson.)

6. Continue to move the handles. When you are happy with the result, click the Arrow. You can change any gradient fill at any time with this tool.

7. Move the Shadow layer to the bottom of the list.

**NOTE**
This would be a good time to save your work or download the project at this point from http://www.phptr.com/essential/flash/stitch/stitch5-12.html.

You have now created the basic components of the splash screen. In the next chapter you will add animation to this scene, create the main page with background animation, and create animated transitions for the main site.

## RECAP

In this chapter you learned how to:
- Reshape an existing graphic
- Use intersections to create more complex shapes
- Use the Brush tool to create free form shapes

## ADVANCED PROJECTS

1. In a new movie, create a rectangular shape with an unusual line style.

2. Change the fill with the Paint Bucket and the Line Style with the Ink Bottle.

3. Use the Arrow to add curves to the sides of the shape.

4. Create brush shapes with gradient fills.

5. Change the fills with the Paint Bucket and the Line Styles with the Ink Bottle.

6. Add and remove curves from the edges of the shapes, using the Arrow tool.

# 6 Advanced Animation

## IN THIS CHAPTER

- Animating Symbols
- Opening Sequence
- Background Music
- Recap
- Advanced Projects

*The* Stitch Fashion Journal *site is intended to be an exciting, glitzy place. The splash screen will be more dramatic than the Shelley animation.*

## ◆ Animating Symbols

In the splash screen, one of the animated effects we will be creating is the rotating button image. The button needs to be made into a symbol and animated. We will be using a new animation technique to accomplish this. Thus far, you have used symbols as graphic objects for tweening; the animation resided in the main scene file. Symbols can also be self-animated. If you wanted to animate the button spinning in the main scene, you would have to tediously rotate it slightly every few frames throughout the entire splash sequence. By self-animating the button, you will be able to create a much smaller sequence with a single rotation, and the button symbol will rotate throughout the splash sequence.

---

**NOTE**

You can download the project at this point from http://www.phptr.com/essential/flash/stitch/stitch5-12.html.

---

### Creating the Button Symbol

1. Select the Button layer.

2. Select the button image.

3. Choose Insert→Convert to Symbol.

4. Name it "Button," and choose Graphic for type (see Figure 6–1). Click OK.

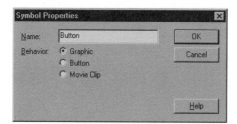

**FIGURE 6–1** Symbol Properties dialog box

5. Deselect the button image.

6. Select the button shadow.

7. Choose Edit→Cut.

8. Select Edit→Edit Symbols.

9. Select the Button symbol from the symbol list to edit. Create a new layer and name it "Button Shadow."

10. Choose Edit→Paste and paste the shadow on the new layer.

11. Select and reposition the shadow as needed.

**12.** Name the original layer "Button Symbol."

**13.** Move the Button Shadow layer under the Button Symbol layer. You should now have two layers for the button symbol in symbol editing mode (see Figure 6–2).

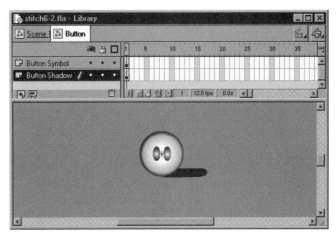

**FIGURE 6–2** Button symbol with two layers

**NOTE**
This would be a good time to save your work or download the project at this point from http://www.phptr.com/essential/flash/stitch/stitch6-1.html.

## Animating the Button

Tweening is usually the easy way to create animations. In the case of the button, it's simpler just to do frame-by-frame animation, since we need just a few frames and we need to exercise tight control over them.

**1.** Begin by selecting the Button layer, and choose Edit→Edit Symbols. You should now be in symbol editing mode.

**2.** Hide the Button Shadow layer using the Layer menu.

**3.** Select the Button Symbol layer.

**4.** Choose View→Snap to turn on Snap to grid.

**5.** Choose Insert→Keyframe to add a new keyframe next to the current one, as shown in Figure 6–3. Select it.

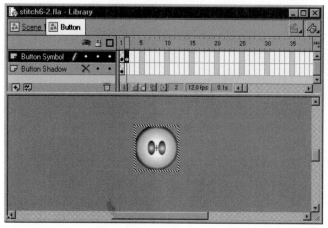

**FIGURE 6–3** Button symbol with keyframe added to Button Symbol layer

**6.** Select the Arrow tool. Choose the Rotate button, as shown in Figure 6–4.

**FIGURE 6–4** Rotate button

**7.** Okay, here's the tricky part. Grab one of the corner handles and rotate the button 45 degrees clockwise (see Figure 6–5).

**FIGURE 6–5** Rotate the button 45 degrees clockwise

8. Insert another keyframe to the right of the current one. Select it.

9. Repeat steps 5, 6, and 7 until the button has been rotated most of the way around. See Figure 6–6 for the progression.

**FIGURE 6–6** Progression of the button rotation

10. You should now have eight keyframes for the button. Press the Enter key to view the animation. Notice that the shadow only appears in the first frame. Let's fix that.

11. Choose Show All from the Layers menu.

12. Select the Button Shadow layer. Click on the eighth frame and choose Insert→Frame (see Figure 6–7). The shadow will now appear in all the frames.

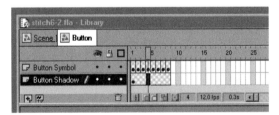

**FIGURE 6–7** Button Shadow layer with eighth frame added

The button is now self-animated. It will appear to rotate throughout the main movie animation.

**NOTE**
This would be a good time to save your work or download the project at this point from http://www.phptr.com/essential/flash/ stitch/stitch6-2.html.

### Creating Other Symbols

A few other graphics on this page need to be turned into symbols.

1. To return to scene editing mode, choose Edit→Edit Movie.

2. If you have any hidden layers, choose Show All from the Layer menu.

3. Select the Fashion Journal text.

4. Choose Insert→Convert to Symbol. Name this "Fashion Text" and leave it as a Graphic. Click OK.

5. Select the photo.

6. Choose Insert→Convert to Symbol. Name this "Photo" and leave it as a Graphic. Click OK.

7. Select the Stitch text.

8. Choose Insert→Convert to Symbol. Name this "Stitch" and leave it as a Graphic. Click OK.

9. Select the needle.

10. Choose Insert→Convert to Symbol. Name this "Needle" and leave it as a Graphic. Click OK.

11. Select the shadow next to the photo.

12. Choose Insert→Convert to Symbol. Name this "Shadow" and leave it as a Graphic. Click OK.

13. Select the Blues text.

14. Choose Insert→Convert to Symbol. Name this "Blues" and leave it as a Graphic. Click OK.

15. Finally, select both pieces of the thread. If they aren't grouped, hold down the Shift key while selecting to get both of them.

16. Choose Insert→Convert to Symbol. Name this "Thread" and leave it as a Graphic. Click OK.

## ◆ Opening Sequence

The animation effects used for the opening sequence are somewhat more elaborate variations of what we used for the Shelley site. You will also be introduced to the motion layer.

## Getting Started

The very first step for creating the splash screen is to decide how long you want the animation to be. The Stitch splash screen lasts 135 frames, which at 12 fps is a little over 11 seconds.

1. Click, hold, and drag the 135th frame of the first layer and drag down to select the 135th frame of all the layers (see Figure 6–8).

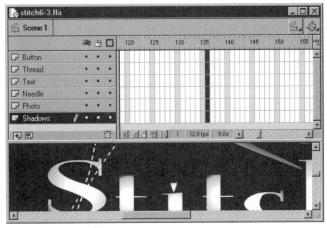

**FIGURE 6–8** 135th layer of all frames selected

2. Turn off Snap by unchecking View→Snap.

3. Choose Insert→Keyframe.

4. We will be working with the button image first, so select the Button layer, and choose Hide Others from the Layer menu.

**NOTE**
This would be a good time to save your work or download the project at this point from http://www.phptr.com/essential/flash/ stitch/stitch6-3.html.

## Moving the Button Image

1. Insert a keyframe at frame 110 of the Button layer.

2. Select the first keyframe of the Button layer.

3. Select the Button symbol with the Arrow and open the Object Inspector by choosing Window→Inspectors→ Object.

4. Change the settings in the Object Inspector to be the same as those in Figure 6–9. Click Apply.

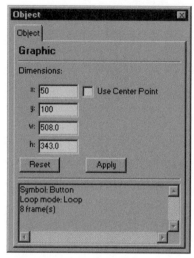

**FIGURE 6–9** Object Inspector dialog box

5. See Figure 6–10, which shows the entire scene, zoomed to 50%.

**FIGURE 6–10** View of the entire scene zoomed to 50%

6. Insert a keyframe at frame 70 of the Button layer.

7. Click on the button image at the first keyframe and select Modify→Instance. This opens the Instance Properties dialog box.

8. Click on the Color Effect tab. Select Alpha from the drop-down list and move the slider to the left to zero, as shown in Figure 6–11. Click OK.

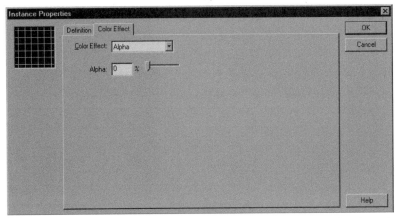

**FIGURE 6–11** Instance Properties dialog box with Color Effect tab selected

9. Double-click on the first keyframe. Select the Tweening tab.

10. Choose the Motion option for Tweening type, set Tween Scaling checked, and Rotate set to Automatic (see Figure 6–12). Click OK.

11. Double-click on the keyframe at 70. Choose the Motion option for Tweening type, set Tween Scaling checked, and Rotate set to Automatic. Click OK.

**NOTE**
This would be a good time to save your work or download the project at this point from http://www.phptr.com/essential/flash/stitch/stitch6-4.html.

That is the complete button animation for the splash screen. Remember: If the location or size of the button isn't quite right at

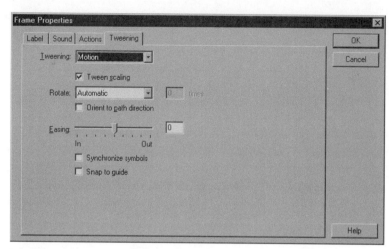

**FIGURE 6–12** Frame Properties dialog box with Tweening tab selected

any point, it can be easily changed. Just click on the keyframe you wish to modify, select the button image with the Arrow, and use the Scale modifier to change it. To test the button animation, press Enter. Notice the rotation that we created in "Animating Symbols."

### Fading in the Thread Image

The thread graphic will fade in, beginning at frame 90 and being completely visible at frame 110.

1. Select the Thread layer and hide the others.

2. Insert keyframes at frame 90 and 110.

3. Select the keyframe at frame 90. Click on the thread symbol.

4. Choose Modify→Instance. You can also double-click on the thread graphic to open this dialog box.

5. Click on the Color Effect tab and slide the Alpha slider to zero.

6. Repeat steps 4 and 5 on the first keyframe. If you prefer, you can simply select and delete the graphic from the first keyframe.

7. Finally, double-click on the keyframe at frame 90 and set the Tweening tab to Motion. Click OK.

**NOTE**
This would be a good time to save your work or download the project at this point from http://www.phptr.com/essential/flash/ stitch/stitch6-5.html.

## Stitch Text Animation and Fading

The Stitch title changes size, fades in and out, and moves around the scene. Instead of setting the tweening at the end of each step, this time you will add it all at once at the end.

1. Choose Show All from the Layer menu.

2. Insert a new layer and name it "Stitch."

3. Click on keyframe 1 of the Text layer.

4. Select the Stitch text and choose Edit→Cut.

5. Select the Stitch layer and hide the others.

6. Click on the first keyframe and choose Edit→Paste in Place.

7. Insert keyframes at frames 10, 20, 70, 95, and 135 (see Figure 6–13).

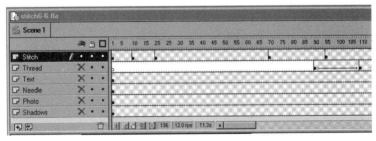

**FIGURE 6–13** Stitch layer with keyframes inserted at frames 10, 20, 70, 95, and 135

8. Select the keyframe at frame 1 and select the Stitch title text. Use the Object Inspector to change the Stitch title to the settings shown in Figure 6–14. Click Apply.

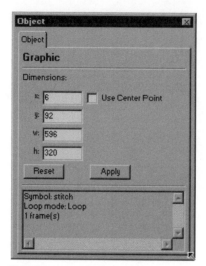

**FIGURE 6–14** Object Inspector dialog box

9. Figure 6–15 shows what the title should look like at the first keyframe.

**FIGURE 6–15** Stitch title at first keyframe

10. Double-click the image at this keyframe.

11. Slide the Alpha to zero on the Color Effect tab of the Instance Properties for the Stitch graphic in this keyframe.

12. Next, select the keyframe at frame 10. Select the Stitch title and use the settings shown in the Object Inspector in Figure 6–16. Click Apply.

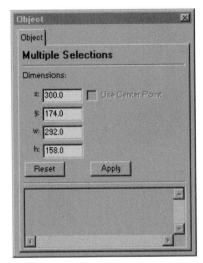

**FIGURE 6–16** Object Inspector dialog box

**13.** The Stitch header should resemble Figure 6–17.

**FIGURE 6–17** Stitch title at keyframe 10

**14.** Select the keyframe at frame 20. Select the Stitch title and use the settings shown in the Object Inspector in Figure 6–18. Click Apply.

**15.** The Stitch header should resemble Figure 6–19.

**16.** Double-click on the image at this keyframe.

**17.** Slide the Alpha to zero on the Color Effect tab of the Instance Properties for the Stitch graphic in this keyframe.

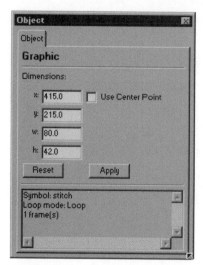

**FIGURE 6–18** Object Inspector dialog box

**FIGURE 6–19** Stitch title at keyframe 20

18. Select the keyframe at frame 70. Use the Arrow and the settings shown in the Object Inspector in Figure 6–20.

19. The Stitch title should look like Figure 6–21.

20. Double-click on the image at this keyframe.

21. Slide the Alpha to zero on the Color Effect tab of the Instance Properties for the Stitch graphic in this keyframe.

22. Finally, change the Tweening property for the keyframes at 1, 10, and 70 to Motion by double-clicking each one in turn and modifying the Tweening tab.

**FIGURE 6–20** Object Inspector dialog box

**FIGURE 6–21** Stitch title at keyframe 70

**NOTE**

This would be a good time to save your work or download the project at this point from http://www.phptr.com/essential/flash/ stitch/stitch6-6.html.

## Fashion Text Animation and Fading

The text Fashion Journal behaves in almost the same way as the Stitch title.

1. Choose Show All from the Layer menu.

2. Insert a new layer and name it "Fashion."

3. Click on keyframe 1 of the Text layer.

4. Select the Fashion Journal text and choose Edit→Cut.

5. Select the Fashion layer and hide the others.

6. Click on the first keyframe and choose Edit→Paste in Place.

7. Insert keyframes at frames 20, 30, 40, 70, 110, and 135.

8. Select the keyframe at frame 1 and delete the Fashion Journal image by selecting it and using Edit→Clear or the Delete key.

9. Select the keyframe at frame 20 and use the Object Inspector to change the Fashion Journal image to the settings in Figure 6–22.

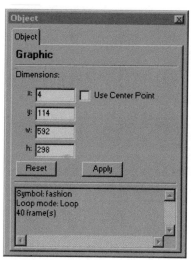

**FIGURE 6–22** Object Inspector dialog box

10. The image should look like Figure 6–23.

11. Double-click on the image at this keyframe.

12. Slide the Alpha to zero on the Color Effect tab of the Instance Properties for the Stitch graphic in this keyframe.

**FIGURE 6–23** Fashion Journal text at keyframe 20

**13.** Select the keyframe at frame 40 and use the Object Inspector to change the Fashion Journal image to the settings in Figure 6–24.

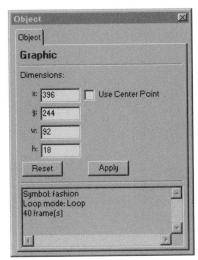

**FIGURE 6–24** Object Inspector dialog box

**14.** The Fashion Journal graphic should look like Figure 6–25.

**15.** Double-click on the image at this keyframe.

**16.** Slide the Alpha to zero on the Color Effect tab of the Instance Properties for the Stitch graphic in this keyframe.

**FIGURE 6–25** Fashion Journal text at keyframe 40

**17.** Select the keyframe at frame 70 and use the Object Inspector to change the Fashion Journal image to the settings in Figure 6–26.

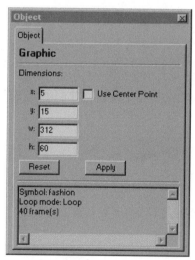

**FIGURE 6–26** Object Inspector dialog box

**18.** The Fashion Journal graphic should look like Figure 6–27.

**19.** Double-click on the image at this keyframe.

**20.** Slide the Alpha to zero on the Color Effect tab of the Instance Properties for the Stitch graphic in this keyframe.

**FIGURE 6–27** Fashion Journal text at keyframe 70

**21.** Finally, change the Tweening property for the keyframes at 20, 30, and 70 to Motion by double-clicking each one in turn and modifying the Tweening tab.

**NOTE**
This would be a good time to save your work or download the project at this point from http://www.phptr.com/essential/flash/ stitch/stitch6-7.html.

## Blues Text with Motion Layer

The Blues text will use a new technique to specify its motion known as a Motion Guide.

**1.** Choose Show All Layers from the Layer menu.

**2.** Rename the Text layer to "Blues."

**3.** Select the Blues layer. Hide the other layers.

**4.** Select the keyframe at 135 and delete the Stitch and Fashion Journal images so that only the Blues text remains.

**5.** Insert a keyframe at frame 110.

**6.** Delete the graphic at keyframe 1.

**7.** Select the keyframe at 110, and use the Object Inspector settings shown in Figure 6–28. Click Apply.

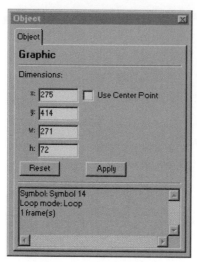

**FIGURE 6–28** Object Inspector dialog box

> **8.** The scene should look like Figure 6–29.

**FIGURE 6–29** Blues text at keyframe 110

> **9.** Choose the Layer menu option Add Motion Guide. A new layer appears above the current Blues layer. Select this new layer.
>
> **10.** Insert a keyframe into this new layer at 110. Select the keyframe at 110.
>
> **11.** Change to the Line tool with the size set to 1.0, the color white, and the style Solid (see Figure 6–30).

**FIGURE 6–30** Line tool with settings

12. Draw a small line from the center of the text up and to the right, as shown in Figure 6–31.

**FIGURE 6–31** Line drawn from the center of text up and to the right

13. Use the Arrow tool to move the ends of this line as needed. The top should be near the center of the Blues text at frame 135. The bottom should be at the center of the Blues text at frame 110 (see Figure 6–32).

14. Using the Arrow tool, click and hold near the middle of the line and drag to the left, as shown in Figure 6–33.

15. Select keyframe 110 of the Blues layer.

16. Double-click the Blues text at this keyframe.

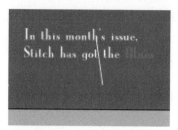

**FIGURE 6–32** Blues text at frame 135

**FIGURE 6–33** Curve added to line

17. Slide the Alpha to zero on the Color Effect tab of the Instance Properties dialog box.

18. The final step is to add motion tweening to keyframe 110 of the Blues layer. The text should now follow that path. The path you created will not show up in the movie you will create. You may wish to hide the motion layer using the Layer menu.

**NOTE**
This would be a good time to save your work or download the project at this point from http://www.phptr.com/essential/flash/stitch/stitch6-8.html.

## Needle Rotation, Fading, and Movement

The needle graphic fades in rapidly while rotating and moving.

1. Select the Needle layer and hide others.

2. Insert keyframes at 70 and 95.

3. Delete the needle image from the keyframe at 1.

4. Select keyframe 70.

5. Use the Arrow tool with the Resize and Rotate buttons to make the needle look like Figure 6–34. The head of the needle is pointed toward the bottom-right corner of the scene.

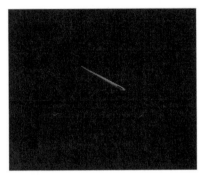

**FIGURE 6–34** Needle appearance at keyframe 70

6. Double-click on the needle image at this keyframe.

7. Slide the Alpha to zero on the Color Effect tab of the Instance Properties.

8. Set motion tweening on frame 70 by double-clicking and setting the Tweening tab.

**NOTE**
This would be a good time to save your work or download the project at this point from http://www.phptr.com/essential/flash/stitch/stitch6-9.html.

## Text Shadow Movement, Shape, and Tint

1. Select the Shadows layer and hide the others.

2. Insert a keyframe at 110 and select it.

3. Change the shape to resemble Figure 6–35. You will need to use the Rotate and Scale settings on the Arrow tool. To make

it a bit more visible while editing it, you may need to change the movie background color by selecting Modify→Movie. A light color will make the shadow more visible.

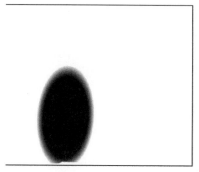

**FIGURE 6–35** Shadow shape at keyframe 110

4. If you changed the movie background, change it back to the original dark blue color.

5. Double-click on the graphic at keyframe 110 to open the Instance Properties dialog box. Select the Color Effect tab.

6. Choose Special from the drop-down list. The Special option allows you to combine both transparency and color hue effects at the same time.

7. Use the settings shown in Figure 6–36. Choose OK.

8. Add motion tweening to keyframe 110 of this layer.

9. The final step is to select the first keyframe and delete the Shadow graphic.

**NOTE**
This would be a good time to save your work or download the project at this point from http://www.phptr.com/essential/flash/stitch/stitch6-10.html.

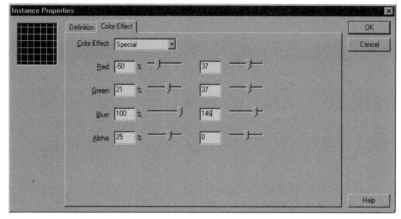

**FIGURE 6–36** Instance Properties dialog box with Color Effect tab selected

## Photograph Fade-in

1. Select the Photo layer and hide others.

2. Insert keyframes at 95 and 110.

3. Select frame 95.

4. Double-click the Photo image at this keyframe.

5. Slide the Alpha to zero on the Color Effect tab of the Instance.

6. Add motion tweening to keyframe 95 of this layer.

7. Select the first keyframe and delete the Photo image.

**NOTE**

This would be a good time to save your work or download the project at this point from http://www.phptr.com/essential/flash/stitch/stitch6-11.html.

We should drag the layers into their proper order. The final order of the layers, from top to bottom, is:

- Button
- Fashion

- Stitch
- Thread
- Guide: Blues
- Blues
- Needle
- Shadows
- Photo

You have now finished the splash screen animation. Time to add some background music!

# ◆ Background Music

You will be creating a new movie that will be called by our *Stitch* splash movie. The movie will consist of a WAV or AIFF file and a switch to turn the music on and off.

### *Creating the New Movie*

1. Choose File→New.

2. Uncheck View→Work Area if it's checked.

3. Select Modify→Movie.

4. Change the movie size to 150 pixels x 30 pixels. Change the background to the same dark blue as you used in the main movie (see Figure 6–37).

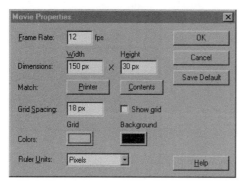

**FIGURE 6–37** Movie Properties settings for new movie

5. Decide on which WAV, AIFF, or mp3 file you wish to use. The one used in the example is stitch.wav and is available as a WAV and AIFF file at http://www.phptr.com/essential/flash/stitch/music/. Smaller file size is definitely preferable.

6. Choose File→Import and locate the file you wish to use.

7. Save this movie as music.fla in the same directory as your splash screen.

**NOTE**
This would be a good time to save your work or download the project at this point from http://www.phptr.com/essential/flash/stitch/music6-1.html.

## Creating the First Button

1. Make sure View→Antialias Text is checked.

2. Choose Window→Library.

3. Click on the Options menu at the right top of this dialog box and choose New Symbol.

4. Name this symbol "Turn Off" and make it a button. Click OK.

5. You are now presented with the symbol editing interface.

6. Using the Text tool, type the words "turn off music" with the font Mona Lisa Solid, or the font of your choice. Use a font size of 20 and white for the color.

7. Select this graphic. Choose Modify→Align.

8. Use the settings shown in Figure 6–38 to center the image. Click OK.

9. Click under the Over frame label and insert a keyframe (see Figure 6–39).

10. Change to the Text tool. Highlight the words. Change the color to a medium gray.

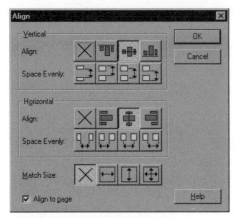

**FIGURE 6–38** Align dialog box

**FIGURE 6–39** Keyframe inserted for Over frame

**NOTE**

This would be a good time to save your work or download the project at this point from http://www.phptr.com/essential/flash/stitch/music6-2.html.

## Creating the Second Button

Creating the second button is very simple.

1. If the Library isn't open, choose Window Library.

2. Click on the Turn Off button in the Library.

3. Click on the Options button at the top right of the Library dialog box and choose Duplicate.

4. Name this new button "Turn On." Change to editing mode for this new button.

5. Change to the Text tool and change the text to read "turn on music." You will need to do this for both the Up and Over keyframes.

**NOTE**
This would be a good time to save your work or download the project at this point from http://www.phptr.com/essential/flash/stitch/music6-3.html.

## Creating the Movie Clip

The sound needs to be embedded with the buttons in a movie clip.

1. If the Library isn't open, choose Window→Library.

2. Click on the Options menu at the right top of this dialog box and choose New Symbol.

3. Name this symbol "Toggle" and make it a movie clip. Click OK.

4. You are now in symbol editing mode for the Toggle movie clip. Add two new layers (see Figure 6–40). You should now have three. Name them "Action," "Button," and "Music."

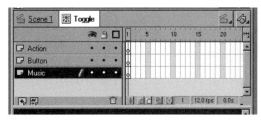

**FIGURE 6–40** Movie with Action, Button, and Music layers

**NOTE**
This would be a good time to save your work or download the project at this point from http://www.phptr.com/essential/flash/stitch/music6-4.html.

### Inserting the Buttons in the Movie

1. Select the Button layer.

2. Insert a keyframe at frame 10. Select the keyframe located at frame 1.

3. In the Library dialog box, click on the Turn Off button you created.

4. Click, hold, and drag the image from the Library to the work area.

5. Center the image, using Modify→Align. You may have to use the scroll bars on the side of the work area to see the center of the window.

6. Select the keyframe located at frame 10.

7. In the Library dialog box, click on the Turn On button you created.

8. Click, hold, and drag the image from the Library to the Scene.

9. Center the image, using Modify→Align.

**NOTE**
This would be a good time to save your work or download the project at this point from http://www.phptr.com/essential/flash/stitch/music6-5.html.

### Modifying the Action Layer

1. Click on the Action layer.

2. Double-click on the keyframe at frame 1 to open the Frame Properties dialog box.

3. On the Label tab, enter "off" for the name. Set the behavior to Label.

4. Change to the Actions tab. Click on the button with the Plus sign and choose Stop (see Figure 6–41). Click OK.

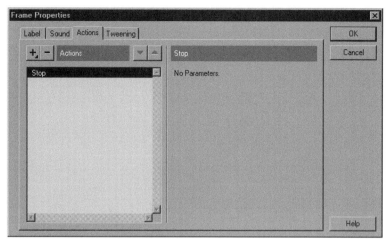

**FIGURE 6–41** Actions tab with Stop action added

5. Insert a keyframe at frame 10 of the Action layer.

6. Double-click on this new keyframe at frame 10 to open the Frame Properties dialog box.

7. On the Label tab, enter "on" for the name. Set the behavior to Label.

8. Change to the Actions tab. Click on the button with the Plus sign and choose Stop. Click OK.

9. You need to add some Instance Properties. Select the keyframe at frame 1 of the Button layer.

10. Using the Arrow, select the Turn Off Music graphic. Choose Modify→Instance.

11. Click on the Actions tab. Choose On MouseEvent from the Plus menu.

12. Check Press from the Parameters on the right (see Figure 6–42).

13. Click on the Plus menu again and this time choose Go To.

14. Change the Frame setting on the right to Label and choose On from the drop-down list (see Figure 6–43). Click OK.

15. You will need to change the Instance Properties for the other button. Select the keyframe at frame 10 of the Button layer.

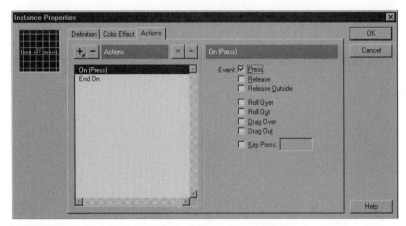

**FIGURE 6–42** Actions tab with On Press event added

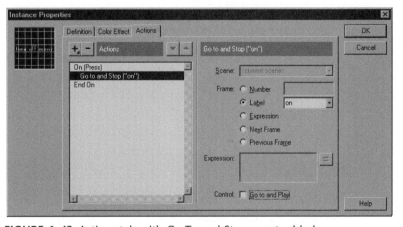

**FIGURE 6–43** Actions tab with Go To and Stop event added

**16.** Using the Arrow, select the Turn On Music graphic. Choose Modify→Instance.

**17.** Click on the Actions tab. Choose On MouseEvent from the Plus menu.

**18.** Check Press from the Parameters on the right.

**19.** Click on the Plus menu again and this time choose Go To.

**20.** Change the Frame setting on the right to Label and choose off from the drop-down list. Click OK.

**NOTE**

This would be a good time to save your work or download the project at this point from http://www.phptr.com/essential/flash/ stitch/music6-6.html.

## Adding the Music Layer

1. Click on the Music layer.

2. Double-click on the keyframe at frame 1.

3. Click on the Sound tab.

4. Choose stitch.wav or stitch.aiff from the Sound drop-down list.

5. Set Effect to None, Sync to Start, and Loops to 9999 (see Figure 6–44). Click OK.

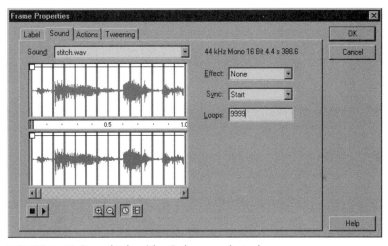

**FIGURE 6–44** Sound tab with stitch.wav selected

6. Insert a keyframe at frame 10 of the Music layer.

7. Double-click on the new keyframe at frame 10.

8. Click on the Sound tab.

9. Choose stitch.wav or stitch.aiff from the Sound drop-down list.

10. Set Effect to None, Sync to Stop, and Loops to 0 (see Figure 6–45). Click OK.

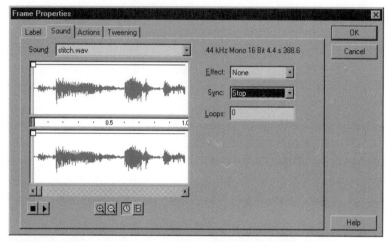

**FIGURE 6–45** Sound tab with Effect, Sync, and Loops set

**NOTE**

This would be a good time to save your work or download the project at this point from http://www.phptr.com/essential/flash/stitch/music6-7.html.

## Adding the Clip to the Movie

Now that you have created the movie clip, it's time to use it in the music movie.

1. Choose Edit→Edit Movie

2. If the Library is not open, choose Window→Library.

3. Select Insert→Layer to add a new layer. Name the two layers "Labels" and "Button."

4. Click on the Labels layer.

5. Insert keyframes at 4, 7, 10, and 20. These keyframes could have been placed right next to each other, but we will space them so that the labels will show up.

6. Double-click on keyframe 1 to open the Frame Properties dialog box.

7. Select the Label tab and name this "1." Set Behavior to Label (see Figure 6–46). Click OK.

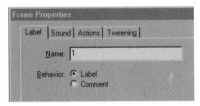

**FIGURE 6–46** Frame Properties dialog box with Label tab selected

8. Double-click on the keyframe at 4 to open the Frame Properties dialog box.

9. Select the Label tab and name this "2." Set Behavior to Label. Click OK.

10. Double-click on the keyframe at 7 to open the Frame Properties dialog box.

11. Select the Label tab and name this "3." Set Behavior to Label. Click OK.

12. Double-click on the keyframe at 10 to open the Frame Properties dialog box.

13. Select the Label tab and name this "loaded." Set Behavior to Label. Click OK. Your Labels layer should now look like Figure 6–47.

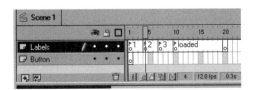

**FIGURE 6–47** Labels layer with label names showing

**14.** Double-click on the keyframe at 4 again.

**15.** Choose the Actions tab.

**16.** Select If Frame Is Loaded from the Plus menu. On the right, choose Label for the Frame setting and choose Loaded from the list box, as shown in Figure 6–48.

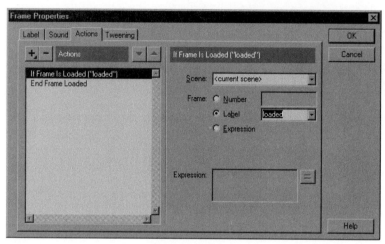

**FIGURE 6–48** Actions tab with If Frame Is Loaded action added

**17.** Choose Go To from the Plus menu. On the right, click Label and choose Loaded from the list box, as shown in Figure 6–49. Click OK.

**18.** Double-click on the keyframe at 7.

**19.** Choose the Actions tab.

**20.** Select If Frame Is Loaded from the Plus menu. On the right, choose Label and 1 from the drop-down list, as shown in Figure 6–50.

**21.** Choose Go To from the Plus menu.

**22.** Click in the Go To and Play check box next to Control. On the right, choose Label and 1 from the drop-down list, as shown in Figure 6–51. Click OK.

**23.** Double-click on the keyframe at 10.

**24.** Choose the Actions tab.

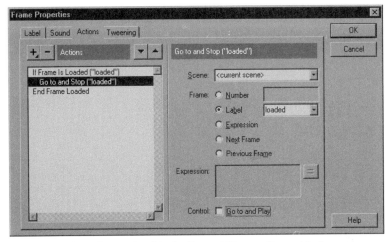

**FIGURE 6–49** Actions tab with Go To and Stop action added

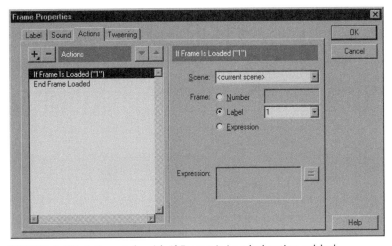

**FIGURE 6–50** Actions tab with If Frame Is Loaded action added

**25.** Select Stop from the Plus menu. Click OK.

**26.** Change to the Button layer. Insert a keyframe at 10 and 20.

**27.** Click on the keyframe at 10. Here is where we actually put the Toggle movie clip.

**28.** Drag the Toggle symbol from the Library window into the scene.

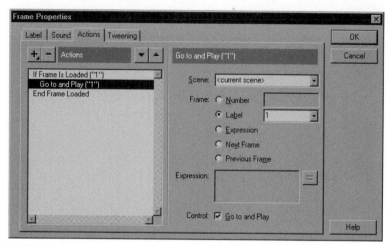

**FIGURE 6–51** Actions tab with Go To and Play action added

**29.** Choose Modify→Align and center the image.

**30.** Select File→Export Movie. Save this as music.swf in the same directory as stitchsplash.fla.

**31.** Change the settings for the Export Flash Player dialog box, as shown in Figure 6–52. Click OK.

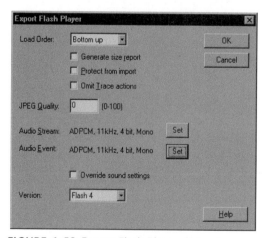

**FIGURE 6–52** Export Flash Player dialog box

**NOTE**

This would be a good time to save your work or download the project at this point from http://www.phptr.com/essential/flash/ stitch/music6-8.html.

## Adding the Clip to the Splash Screen

We have one last task in front of us, and that is to add this to our *Stitch* splash movie.

1. Open the stitchsplash.fla file. This may also be downloaded from http://www.phptr.com/essential/flash/stitch/ stitch6-11.fla.

2. Create a new layer and call it "Music."

3. Double-click on the keyframe at frame 1.

4. On the Actions tab, choose Load/Unload Movie from the Plus menu.

5. For URL, type music.swf. (see Figure 6–53). Click OK.

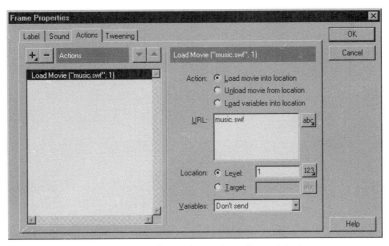

**FIGURE 6–53** Actions tab with Load Movie action added

**NOTE**

This would be a good time to save your work or download the project at this point from http://www.phptr.com/essential/flash/stitch/stitch6-12.html.

Test the movie by selecting Control→Test Movie. You will notice that the toggle is located in the upper-left corner of the scene. This is a default location. If you want to move it, modify the music.fla movie size to match the splash screen size and move the graphic at keyframe 10 of the Button layer wherever you want it.

Now that the splash screen is completed, we will move on to creating more advanced menuing systems and frame actions, a form, and an interactive fashion show.

## RECAP

In this chapter you learned how to:

- Animate symbols
- Create an opening sequence
- Add background music and a button to control it

## ADVANCED PROJECTS

1. Make a copy of the current movie file and change the animation.

2. Modify the motion path of the Blues shadow.

3. Change the music used in the splash screen.

4. Create your own movie and add the music movie to it.

# 7 Advanced Effects

## IN THIS CHAPTER

- Animated Buttons
- Transitions
- Forms
- Interactive Activity
- Recap

*Until now, you have created straightforward animation with no fancy frame actions. In this chapter, you will be shown how to create animated buttons, make a transition from one scene to another, open movies in other browser windows, and stop an animation. You will also be creating a simple comment form and an interactive movie.*

## ◆ Animated Buttons

In this section you will create a button that will be reused throughout the *Stitch* site and in the interactive activity. Instead of having a static graphic for the Over state, the button will play a movie clip.

**NOTE**
You can download the project at this point from http://www.phptr.com/essential/flash/stitch/stitch6-12.html.

### Creating the Parent Button

1. Begin by opening the current stitch.fla file.

2. Select Window→Library to open the symbol library for this file.

3. In the Library dialog box, click the Options button and choose New Symbol.

4. Name this "Parent" and choose type Button. You are presented with the symbol editing screen for your new symbol. It is currently blank.

5. In the Library window, locate the Button symbol. Select it and choose Edit from the Options menu. You will be using this graphic as part of the new Parent button.

6. Select the Button Symbol layer and choose Hide Others from the Layer menu (see Figure 7–1).

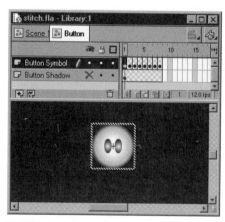

**FIGURE 7–1** Button Symbol layer

7. Select the button image, and choose Edit→Copy.

8. Use the Symbol List button at the top right of the scene to change to the Parent symbol.

9. Click on the Up keyframe and choose Edit→Paste in Place.

10. Open the Object Inspector by choosing Window→ Inspectors→Object.

11. Select the button image in the Up keyframe. Change its location and size to the values shown in Figure 7–2. Click Apply.

**FIGURE 7–2** Object Inspector dialog box

12. Add keyframes for Over and Down.

13. Click on the Down keyframe. Select the button image with the Arrow. Change the Object Inspector values to those shown in Figure 7–3. Click Apply.

## Creating the Movie Clip

Now that the button has been created, you still need to create the movie clip to add to it.

1. Highlight the Button symbol in the Library dialog box.

2. Choose Duplicate from the Options menu.

3. Name the new symbol "Rotation" and make it a movie clip.

4. Use the Symbol List button to change to the Rotation symbol.

**FIGURE 7–3** Object Inspector dialog box

5. We will not be using the button shadow in this movie. Delete the Button Shadow layer on this new symbol by choosing Delete Layer from the Layer menu. Make certain you are deleting the Button Shadow layer, not the Button symbol itself, from the Rotation symbol.

## Adding the Movie Clip to the Button Over State

1. Return to the Parent symbol. Select the Over keyframe.

2. Drag the Rotation movie clip you just created from the Library window onto the work area. You will now have two button images showing.

3. Delete the old one.

4. Select the remaining image. Change its location and size to the values shown in Figure 7–2. Click Apply.

That's it! You have now created an animated button. If you want to test it, open a new blank document and drag the Parent button in it. Then choose Control→Test Movie and check out the mouse states. In the next section you will create the main menu scene, and a transition to it, from the splash animation.

**NOTE**
This would be a good time to save your work or download the project at this point from http://www.phptr.com/essential/flash/ stitch/stitch7-1.html.

# ◆ Transitions

Before you can create a transition from one scene to the next, you need to create a second scene.

### Creating a New Scene

1. Begin by opening the current stitch.fla file if necessary.
2. If you need to do it, choose Edit→Edit Movie to leave Symbol Editing mode.
3. Next choose Window→Inspectors Scene.
4. Click on the Add button on the Scene Inspector, shown in Figure 7–4.

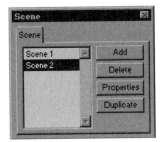

**FIGURE 7–4** Scene Inspector dialog box

5. Click the Properties button for this new scene, Scene 2 (see Figure 7–5). Name this new scene "Menu." Click OK.
6. Since this scene has a name, you should give the original scene a name also. Select Scene 1 and choose Properties.
7. Name this scene "Splash."

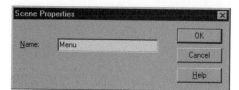

**FIGURE 7–5** Scene Properties dialog box

The Menu scene you will end up with is shown in Figure 7–6. The transition will consist of most of the graphics fading out. The button will roll across the page and then down, leaving a trail of links behind it. The needle will grow larger and move left, and the thread will lengthen.

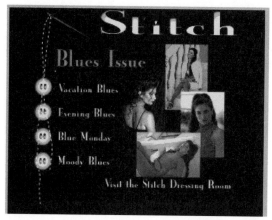

**FIGURE 7–6** Menu scene. (Image ©1999 MJ Wilson.)

### Copying Frames

To do a successful transition from one scene to the next, you need to start the new scene where the old one stopped. So you will be copying the last frame of all the layers of the Splash scene to the first frame of the Menu scene. This sounds more confusing than it is.

1. Make sure the scene currently showing is Splash. You can change scenes with the Scene List button at the top right of the movie window.

2. Click and hold on the last frame on the top layer. This should be the Fashion layer.

3. Drag straight down with the mouse to select the last frame for all the layers at the same time (see Figure 7–7).

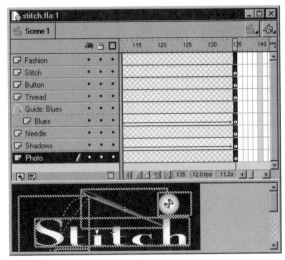

**FIGURE 7–7** Last frame of all layers selected at the same time

4. Right-click (PC) or Ctrl-click (Mac) on the 135th keyframe to open the Layer menu. Choose Copy Frames.

5. Change to the Menu scene. Click on the first keyframe of Layer 1.

6. Open the Layer menu. Choose Paste Frames. For some reason, the paste operation only works in this instance using the Layer menu, and doesn't work when you try the Edit→Paste Frames option. The Menu scene now looks just like the last frame of the Splash scene.

7. Let's remove the music from the Menu scene. Just click on the Music layer and choose Delete Layer from the Layer menu.

8. Finally, we don't need the Blues Text motion guide anymore, so delete this layer also.

**NOTE**
This would be a good time to save your work or download the project at this point from http://www.phptr.com/essential/flash/stitch/stitch7-2.html.

## Fading Out Images

It's time to add the animation for the transition. The first part of the transition consists of most of the images fading out.

1. Select the tenth frame of all the layers and choose Insert→Keyframe.

2. Click on the tenth frame of the Fashion layer. If you are not sure which image you are dealing with, you can select Hide Others from the Layer menu.

3. Click on the Fashion Journal text and choose Modify→ Instance, or double-click the image.

4. Select the Color Effect tab, as shown in Figure 7–8, and choose Alpha. Set the slider to 0%. Click OK.

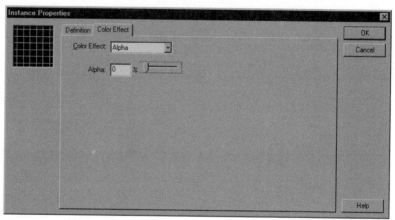

**FIGURE 7–8** Color Effect tab

5. Repeat steps 4 and 5 for the following layers: Blues, Shadows, and Photo. Make sure you have the 10th frame selected when you make the Alpha changes.

---

**NOTE**

This would be a good time to save your work or download the project at this point from http://www.phptr.com/essential/flash/stitch/stitch7-3.html.

---

## Moving and Resizing the Other Images

The images that are still visible at keyframe 10 are the Stitch header, the button, the needle, and the thread. These will all be used as part of the transition animation. Take a look at Figure 7–9 to preview the positions and sizes to which we will be moving these graphics at the 10th frame.

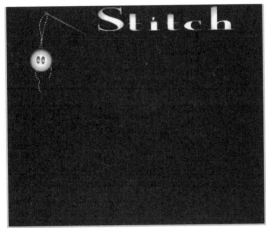

**FIGURE 7–9** Positions and sizes of graphics at 10th frame

1. First, click on the Stitch layer keyframe at frame 10.

2. Open the Object Inspector by choosing Window→Inspectors→Object. Change the values for the Stitch header, as shown in Figure 7–10. Click Apply.

3. Select the needle. To move it up and to the left and make it quite a bit smaller, use the settings in Figure 7–11. Click Apply.

4. Move the thread so it seems to be attached to the eye of the needle.

5. Rotate the thread so it is hanging down, and resize it to resemble Figure 7–12. You may have to move it after rotation to put it back in the needle eye.

6. Use the Object Inspector shown in Figure 7–13 to move the button underneath the needle and make it slightly smaller.

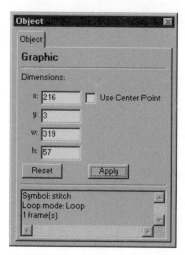

**FIGURE 7–10** Object Inspector dialog box

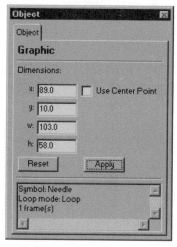

**FIGURE 7–11** Object Inspector dialog box

**7.** Finally, select all frames for all layers by clicking and holding on the top layer and dragging downward and to the right. Select Modify→Frame and change the Tweening tab to Motion, as shown in Figure 7–14.

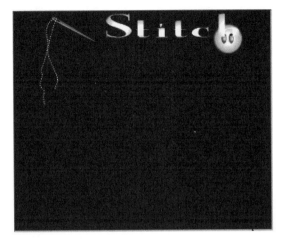

**FIGURE 7–12** Thread rotated to hang down

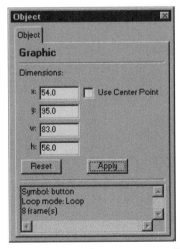

**FIGURE 7–13** Object Inspector dialog box

**NOTE**

This would be a good time to save your work or download the project at this point from http://www.phptr.com/essential/flash/stitch/stitch7-4.html.

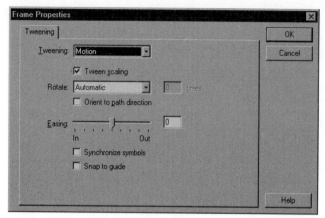

**FIGURE 7–14** Frame Properties dialog box with Tweening tab selected

## Adding More Motion to the Button Symbol

In the transition animation, the Button symbol moves straight down, leaving behind the link buttons.

1. Select the Button layer. You may want to hide the other layers.

2. Add a keyframe at frame 45.

3. Choose View→Work Area.

4. Use the Zoom Control list box on the top toolbar to change the zoom to 50%.

5. Select View→Grid and View→Snap.

6. Select the new keyframe and move the button straight down until it is off the screen.

## Putting in the Link Buttons

The link buttons on this page appear to come from behind the large button as it moves downward.

1. Create a new layer and name it "Links."

2. Drag the new layer to the top of the list. You will be moving it back down after you are done.

3. Use the Layer menu to hide all the layers except for the Links layer.

4. Click on the red X next to the Button layer to make it visible also.

5. Select the Links layer and create a keyframe at 10. Select it.

6. Change to the Text tool and select a light blue color. Select Mona Lisa Solid, or the font of your choice, and a font size of 48.

7. Type the words "Blues Issue."

8. Use the Object Inspector settings shown in Figure 7–15 to resize and move the Blues Issue text. Click Apply.

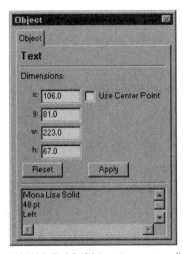

**FIGURE 7–15** Object Inspector dialog box

9. Add a keyframe to the Links layer at frame 15. Select it.

10. Open the Window→Library and select the Parent button from the list.

11. Drag the image from the Library to the scene and place it on top of the larger button, as shown in Figure 7–16.

12. Insert a keyframe at frame 20 of the Links layer and drag another Parent button on the scene, as shown in Figure 7–17.

13. Create keyframes at 25 and 30 and repeat this process for each. Keyframe 30 should look like Figure 7–18.

**FIGURE 7–16** Button placed on top of larger button at frame 15

**FIGURE 7–17** Button placed on top of larger button at frame 20

   **14.** Insert a final keyframe at 45.

   **15.** The Blues Issue text will be animated to come out from behind the button and will grow when we reorganize the layers. Select the keyframe at 10.

   **16.** Select the Blues Issue text. Use the settings shown in Figure 7–19. This will resize and move the text so that it is completely on top of the button. Click Apply.

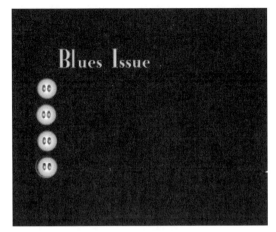

**FIGURE 7–18** All four buttons placed

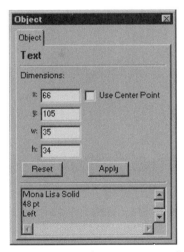

**FIGURE 7–19** Object Inspector dialog box

**17.** Double-click keyframe 10 to open the Frame Properties dialog box. Click on the Tweening tab and change the Tweening to Motion. Click OK.

**18.** Finally, drag the Links layer down to the bottom of the layer list. One important thing: Make sure the only keyframe in this layer with tweening set is 10. The rest should all have tweening set to none.

**NOTE**
This would be a good time to save your work or download the project at this point from http://www.phptr.com/essential/flash/ stitch/stitch7-5.html.

## Adding the Articles and Photos

The article text and photos are static. They are in their own layer and simply appear at frame 15.

1. Insert and select a new layer, called "Articles."

2. Choose Hide Others from the Layer menu.

3. Click on the red X next to the Links layer to make it visible also.

4. Insert a keyframe at frame 15 of the Articles layer.

5. If necessary, click on frame 45 and choose Insert→Frame.

6. Select the keyframe at 15 of the Articles layer.

7. Change to the Text tool. Use Mona Lisa Solid or the font of your choice, font color white. Enter a font size of 26 in the font size box.

8. Enter the article names, as shown in Figure 7–20. Don't worry about their locations; we will move them shortly.

9. Select the frame at 30 and move the article names next to the buttons, as shown in Figure 7–21. The article names are "Vacation Blues," "Evening Blues," "Blue Monday," and "Moody Blues." Don't move the buttons, just the article text. Select View→Grid and View→Snap and increase the zoom amount to assist in lining up the links.

10. Select keyframe 15 of the Articles layer again.

11. Choose File→Import to select the four photos and place them on the page (see Figure 7–22).

12. The imported images can be resized with the Arrow tool, using the Scale option. They can be reordered using the Modify→Arrange options. The photos used on the sample

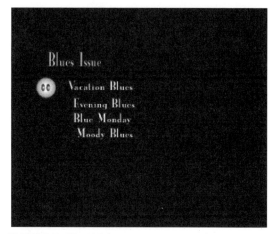

**FIGURE 7–20** Article names

**FIGURE 7–21** Article names moved next to buttons

site can be downloaded from http://www.phptr.com/
essential/flash/stitch/misc/photos.html.

**NOTE**

This would be a good time to save your work or download the
project at this point from http://www.phptr.com/essential/flash/
stitch/stitch7-6.html.

**FIGURE 7–22** Four photos placed on scene. (Image ©1999 MJ Wilson.)

### Lengthening the Thread

You have only one last animation step, stretching out the thread.

1. Choose Show All from the Layer menu.

2. Insert a keyframe at 45 for any layers that do not have one.

3. Select keyframe 45 of the Thread layer. Click on the thread graphic with the Arrow. Turn on the Scale option.

4. Drag the thread downward until it is long enough to reach the bottom of the page. You will have to move the thread to line up with the eye of the needle again. See Figure 7–6 for a better idea of what it should look like.

Now that you have two scenes, your movie will display the splash scene animation, followed by the second, but then it will display the first scene again. It is very important that you tell the Flash player to stop at the end of the Menu scene.

### Stopping the Action at the End of the Menu Scene Animation

Here's how to set a stop action at the end of the Menu scene.

1. Choose any one of the keyframes at 45. It does not matter which layer you choose. The example site uses the Articles layer.

2. Choose Modify→Frame. Select the Actions tab.

**3.** From the Plus menu, choose Stop, as shown in Figure 7–23. Click OK. Now the player will stop at that frame.

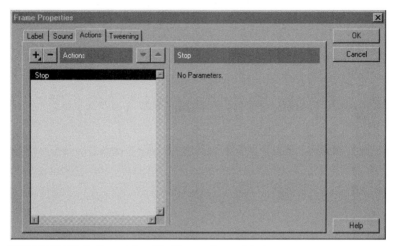

**FIGURE 7–23** Actions tab with Stop action added

**NOTE**
This would be a good time to save your work or download the project at this point from http://www.phptr.com/essential/flash/stitch/stitch7-7.html.

Since you have already learned how to call other pages with button actions in Chapter 3, we won't cover that in detail here. Remember: To add a link to a button, simply set its Action to Get URL and specify a page on the right. In this case, you should double-click each of the buttons in keyframe 45 to access its Instance Property dialog box and use that Action tab.

Now that the drudge work of creating a menu page is out of the way, it's time to create a simple comment form with Flash.

## ◆ Forms

This section will show you how to create an extremely simple Flash 4 form for soliciting comments from visitors to the *Stitch* site. The form consists of two text fields, a subject and comments box. When the Submit button is clicked, the form is e-mailed to an e-mail embedded in the button action. Although the form presented here doesn't interact with a CGI script, it can easily be modified to do so.

### Creating the Form

The comment form is very simple, consisting of a title, two text fields with labels, and an OK button. Figure 7–24 shows you what the form will look like.

**FIGURE 7–24** Stitch comment form

1. You'll need to create a new movie. Choose File→New.

2. Choose Modify→Movie. Change the movie size to 600 pixels by 500 pixels.

3. Change the background color to the same dark blue used for the *Stitch* site. Click OK.

4. Change to the Rectangle tool (see Figure 7–25). Set the line color to be transparent, and the fill to a medium gray.

5. Draw a small rectangle.

6. If the Object Inspector is not open, choose Window→ Inspectors→Object.

**FIGURE 7–25** Rectangle tool with settings

7. Use the Arrow to select the rectangle you just created.

8. Change the location and size to the settings shown in Figure 7–26. Click Apply.

9. Change to the Text tool. Choose Mona Lisa Solid or the font of your choice, a font size of 36, and white for the color.

10. Type the phrase "Stitch Comment Form."

11. Change to a font size of 20.

12. Type the words "Subject" and "Body."

13. Look at the Text tool settings. At the very bottom, shown in Figure 7–27, is the Text Input Box setting. Select this. When you use the Text tool, you will draw a text input box.

14. Draw two input boxes. The font selection and size will be what appears in the box when the form is used in a browser.

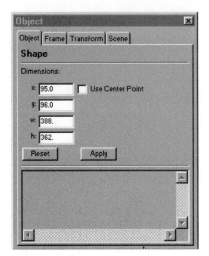

**FIGURE 7–26** Object Inspector dialog box

**FIGURE 7–27** Text tool settings

**15.** Reposition and resize the items on the page to resemble the screen shot in Figure 7–24. We need only add the Submit button.

**16.** Flash 4 has some premade form controls. To use their premade button for the form, choose Libraries→Buttons.

**17.** Select Push Button from the list and drag it onto the work area. Change to symbol editing mode and add the world "OK" to the button.

## Setting the Variables

The next step is to assign the values of the text boxes to variables. When the form is submitted, these are the values that will be sent to the mail message.

1. Select the top text input box and right-click (PC) or Ctrl-click (Mac) and choose Properties.

2. Type "subject" for the Variable value. Choose Draw border and background under Options and select the Do not include font outlines option (see Figure 7–28). Click OK. The Outlines setting is used to tells Flash which characters to include as antialiased graphics. Using these increases the file size. The specified outline options restrict the characters that can be entered into the text area.

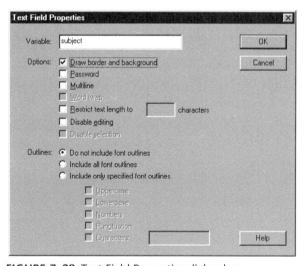

**FIGURE 7–28** Text Field Properties dialog box

3. Select the second text input box and right-click (PC) or Ctrl-click (Mac) and choose Properties.

4. Type "body" for the Variable value. Choose Draw border and background under Options and select the Do not include font outlines, Multiline, and Word Wrap options. Click OK.

## Creating a New Scene

We need to create another scene that can be displayed when the message is sent.

1. Choose Insert→Scene.

2. Change to the new scene with the Scene List button.

3. Use the Text tool to type "Thanks for your comments." Make this fairly large and centered.

## Adding the Actions

1. Return to the first scene.

2. We need to add a Stop action to this scene so that the movie will not play the second scene automatically. Double-click the keyframe. Choose the Actions tab and select Stop from the Plus menu. Click OK.

3. Select the OK button on the form.

4. Choose Modify→Instance. Select the Actions tab.

5. Choose On MouseEvent from the Plus menu. Select Press for the Event on the right.

6. Choose Get URL. On the right, enter mailto:lynn@rainc.com where lynn@rainc.com is the e-mail address you want this form to be sent to (see Figure 7–29).

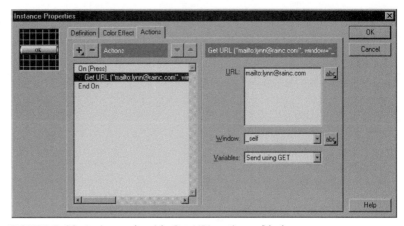

**FIGURE 7–29** Actions tab with Get URL action added

7. Select _self for Window and Send, using GET for Variables.

8. We need to tell the button to change to the other scene when it is pressed. Choose Go To from the Plus menu.

9. On the right side of the tab choose Scene 2 for Scene and Frame Number 1 (see Figure 7–30.). Click OK.

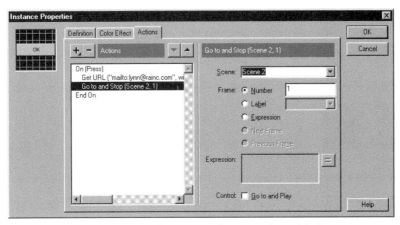

**FIGURE 7–30** Actions tab with Go To and Stop action added

That's it! To publish, you need to create an HTML and a Flash file under Formats in the Publish Settings. This is a very simple form that may not work on all browsers. The point here is that variables can be sent using POST or GET to another URL with the Get URL action on the button. The URL can be the location of a script, where the variables can be parsed and used.

**NOTE**

This would be a good time to save your work or download the project at this point from http://www.phptr.com/essential/flash/stitch/form7-1.html.

We will now move on to the interactive activity planned for this site: a virtual dressing room!

## ◆ Interactive Activity

Since *Stitch* is a fashion site, it makes sense that they would be interested in selling clothes. The *Stitch* dressing room is an interactive page that lets the viewer change the color of the clothes being displayed. Figure 7–31 will give you an idea of what the first part of the final movie will look like.

**FIGURE 7–31** Stitch dressing room. (Image ©1999 MJ Wilson.)

### *Getting Started*

This interactive activity is not part of the other movie. You will need to create a new movie.

1.  Choose File→New.

2.  By default, text antialiasing is off. Turn it on by selecting View→Antialias Text.

3.  Get out of the work area view mode by unchecking View→Work Area.

4.  Choose Modify→Movie, and make the movie size 600 pixels x 500 pixels.

5.  Set the background color to the same blue as you used in the other movie: first column, third row in the Color dialog box. Click OK.

6. Select File→Open as Library and choose the most recent stitch.fla. This opens only the Library dialog box associated with the file.

7. Save the new file as room.fla.

**NOTE**

This would be a good time to save your work or download the project at this point from http://www.phptr.com/essential/flash/stitch/room7-1.html.

The entire activity consists of two frames, each of which contains four buttons (each with a different color), four photos, Previous and Next buttons, and some static graphics. Unlike previous movies you've created, this one does not have any animation. Rather, the photograph changes when one of the buttons is pressed.

## Adding the Static Elements

1. Type the words "Stitch Dressing Room" with the Text tool, using the same font you used for the main site, font size of 24, and a white color.

2. Using the same settings, type the word "Previous" and the word "Next." These should be separate text items.

3. Select the Previous label and choose Insert→Convert to Symbol. Name it "Previous" and make it a button.

4. Select the Next label and choose Insert→Convert to Symbol. Name it "Next" and make it a button.

5. Using the Library dialog box for stitch.fla, which you opened earlier, find the Needle graphic.

6. Drag the Needle image into the scene.

7. Open the Object Inspector and change the values for the Needle image to those shown in Figure 7–32. Click Apply.

8. Change the *Stitch* Dressing Room text location and size to the values shown in Figure 7–33. Click Apply.

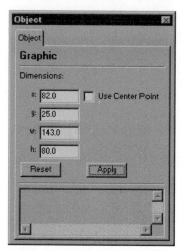

**FIGURE 7–32** Object Inspector dialog box

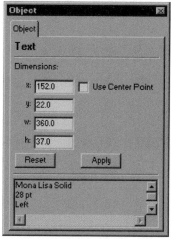

**FIGURE 7–33** Object Inspector dialog box

9. Drag the Thread symbol into the scene. It will need to be resized and rotated by hand to match the screen shot in Figure 7–31.

10. Move the Next and Previous buttons to the approximate locations shown.

11. Insert a keyframe at frame 2.

12. Close the stitch.fla Library window.

## Creating a Movie Clip

Instead of calling each photo when the appropriate button is pressed, call a particular frame in a movie clip.

1. Choose Window→Library to open the Library for the current dialog box.

2. From the Options menu on the Library, choose New Symbol.

3. Name it "Colors" and make it a movie clip. Click OK.

4. Insert three keyframes right next to each other (see Figure 7–34).

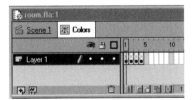

**FIGURE 7–34** Three keyframes added to Layer 1

5. Download the following files from http://www.phptr.com/ essential/flash/stitch/misc/room/: aqua1.jpg, blue1.jpg, ivory1.jpg, yellow1.jpg, blue2.jpg, gold2.jpg, green2.jpg, and red2.jpg

6. Click on the first keyframe. Choose File→Import and locate aqua1.jpg.

7. Click on the second keyframe and import ivory1.jpg.

8. Click on the third keyframe and import blue1.jpg.

9. Click on the fourth one and import yellow1.jpg.

10. Return to the first keyframe and choose Modify Frame.

11. Choose the Label tab, and name it "aqua," as shown in Figure 7–35. The Behavior should be Label. Click OK.

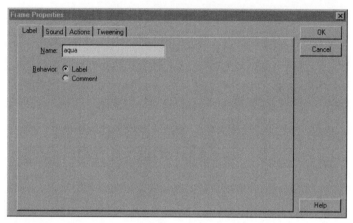

**FIGURE 7–35** Frame Properties with Label tab selected

12. Repeat this labeling for the other three images, naming them, in order, "ivory," "blue," and "yellow."

**NOTE**
This would be a good time to save your work or download the project at this point from http://www.phptr.com/essential/flash/stitch/room7-3.html.

### Adding the Colored Buttons

1. Choose Edit→Edit Movie. Select the first keyframe.

2. Select File→Open as Library and choose stitch.fla.

3. Find the Parent button in the Library.

4. Drag four instances of the Parent button into the scene (see Figure 7–36).

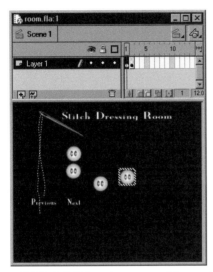

**FIGURE 7–36** Four instances of Parent button in the scene

5. Line them up on the thread, as shown earlier in Figure 7–31. Use the Grid and Snap options as well as the Align dialog box to assist you.

6. Change to the second keyframe and drag four instances into this frame as well. Line them up.

7. Return to the first keyframe and double-click on the top button.

8. Click on the Color Effect tab.

9. Choose Tint from the drop-down box.

10. Change the color to 36, 242, 210, and the Tint Amount to 40%, as shown in Figure 7–37. Click OK.

11. Repeat the process for the second button, choosing 243, 255, 193, and 40%.

12. Change the third and fourth buttons also. The third button should be colored 98, 217, 247. The fourth should be 251, 251, 77. Use 40% for both.

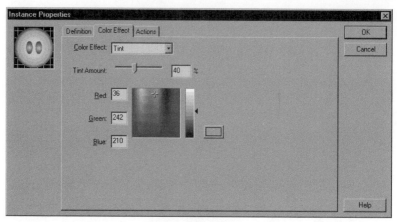

**FIGURE 7–37** Color Effect tab for top button

13. Change to the second keyframe. Change the color of the first button to 73, 152, 248 and the Tint Amount to 40%.

14. Change the second, third and fourth buttons also. The second button should be colored 233, 222, 107. The third button should be colored 81, 232, 53. The fourth should be 208, 40, 41. Use 40% for all three.

**NOTE**

This would be a good time to save your work or download the project at this point from http://www.phptr.com/essential/flash/stitch/room7-4.html.

### Adding Some Text Labels

1. Select the first keyframe. Use the Text tool to add the color labels next to each button, as shown in Figure 7–38.

2. Align the text labels so that they line up with the buttons.

3. Select the second keyframe and add the labels shown in Figure 7–39.

4. Move the text labels so that they line up with the buttons.

**FIGURE 7–38** Color labels added to each button for first keyframe

**FIGURE 7–39** Color labels added to each button for second keyframe

## Applying the Action to the First Button

Each one of the buttons will call a particular frame of the movie you created.

1. Select the first keyframe and drag an instance of the Colors movie onto the work area from the Library dialog box.

2. Double-click on this movie instance you just created to open the Instance Properties dialog box for it.

3. Choose the Definition tab.

4. Set the Instance Name to Suit. Leave the Behavior set to Movie Clip (see Figure 7–40). Click OK.

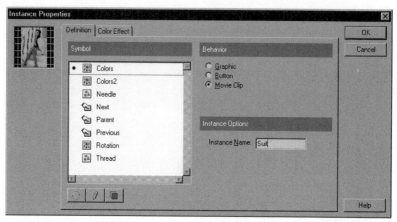

**FIGURE 7–40** Definition tab for movie instance. (Image ©1999 MJ Wilson.)

5. Double-click on the Aqua button with the Ocean label next to it. This is the top button on the first keyframe.

6. Choose the Actions tab.

7. Select On MouseEvent from the Plus menu.

8. On the right of the dialog box, click in the Press and Release check boxes, as shown in Figure 7–41.

9. Now choose Tell Target from the Plus menu.

10. On the right of the dialog box, you will see Suit in the box. Double-click it to select it.

11. Choose Go To from the Plus menu.

12. Click in the Label radio button and type in "aqua," as shown in Figure 7–42. Click OK.

**NOTE**
This would be a good time to save your work or download the project at this point from http://www.phptr.com/essential/flash/stitch/room7-5.html.

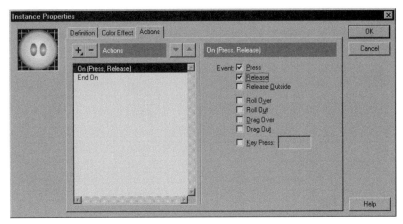

**FIGURE 7–41** Actions tab with On MouseEvent action added

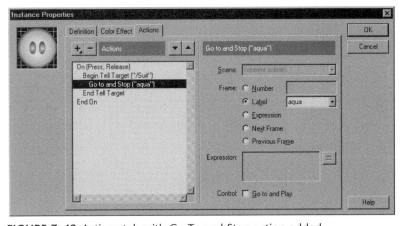

**FIGURE 7–42** Actions tab with Go To and Stop action added

## Applying the Action to the Second Button

1. Double-click on the second button in the first keyframe.

2. Choose the Actions tab.

3. Select On MouseEvent from the Plus menu.

4. On the right of the dialog box, click in the Press and Release check boxes.

5. Now choose Tell Target from the Plus menu.

6. On the right of the dialog box, you will see Suit in the box. Double-click it to select it. The Target box on the right should now read /Suit.

7. Choose Go To from the Plus menu.

8. Click in the Label radio button and type in "ivory," as shown in Figure 7–43. Click OK.

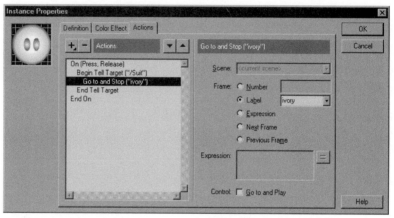

**FIGURE 7–43** Actions tab with Go To and Stop action added

## Applying Actions to the Third and Fourth Buttons

Repeat steps 1 through 9 for the third and fourth buttons. The only difference for each button is step 8. The Label for step 8 should be blue for the third button and yellow for the fourth.

**NOTE**

This would be a good time to save your work or download the project at this point from http://www.phptr.com/essential/flash/stitch/room7-6.html.

## Setting Actions for the First Keyframe

If you tried to play the movie right now, all it would do is keep playing, swapping between the two frames. We need to apply some actions to the keyframes.

1. Double-click the first keyframe, or choose Modify→Frame.

2. Select the Label tab and enter the name "Suit." Choose Label for the Behavior setting.

3. Click on the Actions tab.

4. Choose Stop from the Plus menu.

5. Next, choose Tell Target.

6. Double-click on the Suit label on the right.

7. Now choose Go To and click on the Number radio button for Frame.

8. Put the number 1 in the Frame blank (see Figure 7–44). Click OK.

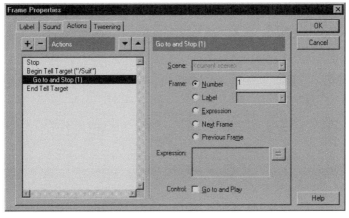

**FIGURE 7–44** Actions tab with Go To and Stop action added

## Creating the Movie Clip for the Second Keyframe

To put together the second keyframe, you will need another movie clip.

1. Choose Window→Library to open the Library.

2. From the Options menu on this dialog box, choose New Symbol.

3. Name it "Colors2" and make it a movie clip. Click OK.

4. Insert three keyframes right next to each other.

5. Click on the first keyframe. Choose File→Import and choose blue2.jpg.

6. Click on the second keyframe and import gold2.jpg.

7. Click on the third keyframe and import green2.jpg.

8. Click on the fourth one and import red2.jpg.

9. Return to the first keyframe and double-click on it.

10. Choose the Label tab, and name it "blue."

11. Repeat for the other three images, naming them, in order, "gold," "green," and "red."

**NOTE**
This would be a good time to save your work or download the project at this point from http://www.phptr.com/essential/flash/stitch/room7-7.html.

### Applying the Action to the First Button

Each of the buttons will call a particular frame of the movie you created. For example, when the viewer is looking at the suit page and the Lemon button is pressed, the image should change to the frame of the Colors movie clip containing the yellow suit image.

1. Choose Edit→Edit Movie. Select keyframe 2.

2. Drag an instance of the Color2 movie from the Library dialog box onto keyframe 2 of the scene.

3. Double-click on the movie instance you just created.

4. Choose the Definition tab.

5. Set the Instance Name to Shirt (see Figure 7–45). Click OK.

6. Double-click on the blue button with the text label Denim next to it.

7. Choose the Actions tab.

8. Select On MouseEvent from the Plus menu.

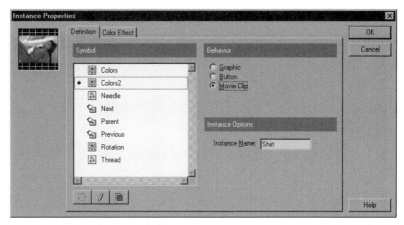

**FIGURE 7–45** Definition tab for movie instance. (Image ©1999 MJ Wilson.)

**9.** On the right of the dialog box, click in the Press and Release check boxes, as shown in Figure 7–46.

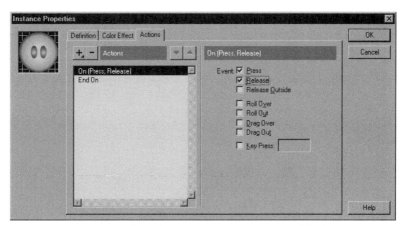

**FIGURE 7–46** Actions tab with On MouseEvent action added

**10.** Now choose Tell Target from the Plus menu.

**11.** On the right of the dialog box, you will see Shirt in the box. Double-click it to select it.

**12.** Choose Go To from the Plus menu.

**13.** Click in the Label radio button and type in "blue," as shown in Figure 7–47. Click OK.

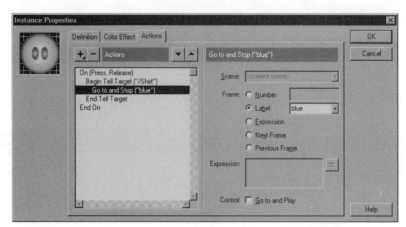

**FIGURE 7–47** Actions tab with Go To and Stop action added

In order to apply actions to the second, third, and fourth buttons, repeat steps 7 through 13 for the second, third, and fourth buttons. The Label for step 8 should be gold for the second button, green for the third button, and red for the fourth.

---

**NOTE**

This would be a good time to save your work or download the project at this point from http://www.phptr.com/essential/flash/stitch/room7-8.html.

---

### Setting Actions for the Second Keyframe

1. Double-click the second keyframe, or choose Modify→ Frame.

2. Select the Label tab and enter the name "Shirt."

3. Click on the Actions tab.

4. Choose Stop from the Plus menu.

5. Next, choose Tell Target.

6. Double-click on the Shirt label on the right.

7. Now choose Go To and click on the Number radio button for Frame.

8. Put the number 2 in the Frame blank (see Figure 7–48). Click OK.

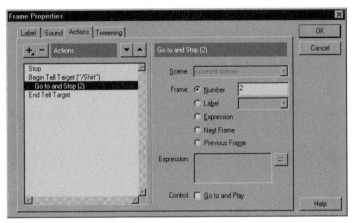

**FIGURE 7–48** Actions tab with Go To and Stop action added

## Adding Next and Previous Buttons

The final thing for the activity to work is the addition of the Next and Previous actions. Since you only have two frames, the Next and Previous buttons will both point to the same thing on the frame. On keyframe 1, they will both call the second frame, which you named "Shirt." On keyframe 2, they will both call the first frame, which you called "Suit." Obviously if you had more frames you would have to change where they pointed.

1. Click on the first keyframe.

2. Use the Arrow to select the Next button.

3. Select Modify→Instance.

4. Change to the Actions tab.

5. Choose On MouseEvent from the Plus menu.

6. On the right, select the Release check box (see Figure 7–49).

7. Choose Go To from the Plus menu.

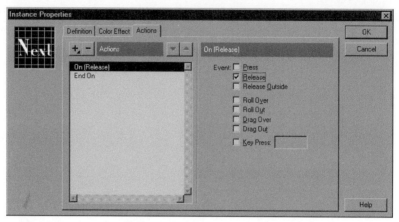

**FIGURE 7–49** Actions tab with On MouseEvent action added

8. On the right, select Label and enter "Shirt" in the blank. Click OK.

9. Select the Previous button and follow steps 3 through 8.

10. Change to the second keyframe.

11. Use the Arrow to select the Next button.

12. Select Modify→Instance.

13. Change to the Actions tab.

14. Choose On MouseEvent from the Plus menu.

15. On the right, select the Release check box.

16. Choose Go To from the Plus menu.

17. On the right, select Label and enter "Suit" in the blank. Click OK.

18. Select the Previous button and follow steps 12 through 17.

**NOTE**
This would be a good time to save your work or download the project at this point from http://www.phptr.com/essential/flash/stitch/room7-9.html.

You have finished! To test the activity, choose Control→Test Movie. Uh-oh . . . you forgot one thing—a link to this movie from the main site!

1. Open the latest stitch.fla.

2. Choose the Menu scene from the Scene List button on the top right.

3. Select the Links layer and choose its last keyframe.

4. Use the Text tool to type "Visit the Stitch Dressing Room." The font is Mona Lisa Solid, font size is 24, and color is white.

5. Select the text with the Arrow tool and choose Insert→ Convert to Symbol.

6. Name it "Visit" and make it a button.

7. Select it and choose Edit→Edit Symbols.

8. Insert a keyframe on Over.

9. Select the text, change to the Text tool, and change the color to light blue.

10. Insert a keyframe on Down. Double-click this keyframe.

11. Choose the Actions tab and select Get URL from the Plus menu. Enter room.html for the URL on the right and choose _blank for the target window (see Figure 7–50). Click OK.

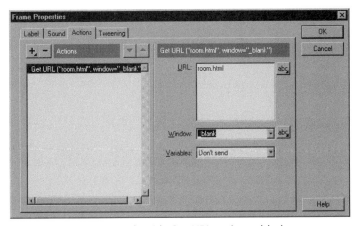

**FIGURE 7–50** Actions tab with Get URL action added

If you were using frames, you could control which frame is loaded on button clicks by using this technique and changing the Window setting.

**NOTE**

This would be a good time to save your work or download the project at this point from http://www.phptr.com/essential/flash/stitch/stitch7-8.html.

## Final Production: Publishing

You called room.html in the preceding button action, but that file does not yet exist. For that matter, the stitch.fla file has not yet been made into a movie. Let's fix that.

1. Open both room.fla and stitch.fla.

2. Choose File→Publish Settings for each. Both will need an HTML and a Flash file created under the Formats tab. For the most part, the default values should be used. You may want to play with the JPEG compression setting to achieve a middle ground between reasonable file size and reasonable image quality.

Test your movies in your Web browser and play with the Publish settings. You may prefer to set the movie size to match the browser rather than the movie file. These files may take a little while to download over a network.

You have now learned all the essentials of Flash 4 creation and production. Flash is an extremely powerful Web tool, and its use is limited only by your imagination.

## RECAP

In this chapter you learned how to:
- Create animated buttons
- Make a transition from one scene to another
- Open movies in other browser windows
- Create a comment form
- Create an interactive movie

# A  Flash 4 Reference

## ACTIONS

Actions are behaviors that can be assigned to frames. These can be triggered by specific events. To access the Actions interface, choose Modify→Frame and select the Actions tab. Click on the button with the Plus sign. These are the possible actions:

**Go To** is used to make the movie go to another frame, scene, or movie.

**Play and Stop** are used to control the current movie.

**Toggle High Quality** turns antialiasing on or off.

**Stop All Sounds** stops any sounds being played by the movie.

**Get URL** is used to make buttons or frames fetch a particular URL. It also allows you to specify a frame in which the new URL can appear.

The **FS Command** action is used to communicate with the program hosting the Flash player, such as a browser or stand-alone projector.

**Load/Unload Movie** loads or unloads a movie located at the specified URL. Loaded movies can be given level numbers or expressions with this action type to allow identification and ordering.

**Tell Target** creates a program block used for sending commands to an instance of a symbol or movie. The instance must be given a label name, and the Tell Target must be given this name.

**If Frame Is Loaded** creates an IF program block used for executing commands if the named frame has been loaded.

**On MouseEvent** is an action used by button instances. When the specified mouse action takes place, the commands are carried out.

**If** creates an expression to be evaluated and a program block that is executed if the condition is met.

**Loop** creates an expression to be evaluated and a program block that is executed until the condition is no longer met.

**Call** can be used to call a frame and execute its actions.

**Set Property** allows you to change one of the properties of a target.

**Set Variable** allows you to set or modify the value of a variable.

**Duplicate/Remove Movie Clip** allows you to duplicate or remove clips. Duplicate allows you to specify the target, give the movie a new name, and give it a depth value.

**Drag Movie Clip** causes the movie clip instance specified by the target movie to follow the mouse cursor as it is moved.

**Trace** is used to track the value of variables, specifically for debugging. A window opens and displays the specified values.

**Comment** is used to add a comment at any point to the Action code you have created.

## ALIGN

The Align dialog box is used to align or match the sizes of more than one object (see Figure A–1).The Align dialog box can also use to evenly distribute the space between groups of objects.

## ANTIALIAS

Antialias is a display mode that smoothes the edges of lines and shapes. It can be toggled on or off using the menu option View→Antialias.

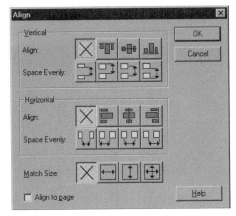

**FIGURE A–1** The Align dialog box

## ANTIALIAS TEXT

Antialias Text is a display mode that smoothes the edges of text created in Flash. It can be toggled on or off using the menu option View→Antialias Text.

## ARRANGE

The menu option Modify→Arrange is used to access several ordering commands. These commands are used to change the order of graphic objects and text within a single layer.

## ARROW

The Arrow tool is used to select, move, scale, and rotate graphics. It can also be used to add and modify curves on lines and shapes. To select multiple objects, use the Arrow and the Shift key. When an object is selected, clicking on it and dragging will move it. When the Scale or Rotate button is on, the currently selected object can be scaled or rotated by using the handles. The Smooth and Straighten buttons can be used to smooth or straighten curved lines. Finally, when the Arrow is placed on an unselected line or the edge of a shape and the cursor changes, clicking and dragging will curve the object.

## BREAK APART

Modify→Break Apart ungroups grouped objects, text objects, symbols, bitmaps, and OLE objects. This makes it possible to edit parts of these objects.

## BRUSH

The Brush tool is used to create free-form images. The Brush controls include:

> **Brush Mode**, which controls what can be painted. Paint Normal applies the brush anywhere. Paint Fills applies the brush only to other fills, leaving lines alone. Paint Behind paints only on empty areas. Paint Selection applies the brush to selected fills only. Paint Inside paints only over the inside fill at the place where you begin painting.
>
> **Fill Color** controls the color that the brush paints. This may also be a gradient fill.
>
> **Brush Size** is used to set the size of the brush stroke.
>
> **Brush Shape** is used to set the shape of the brush stroke.

## CONTROLLING MOVIES

The Menu option Control contains several commands for testing the movie being created.

> **Play** plays the current movie in the scene from the current frame to the end.
>
> **Rewind** returns to the first keyframe.
>
> **Step Forward** sets the current frame to the next in sequence.
>
> **Step Backward** sets the current frame to the previous in sequence.
>
> **Test Movie** plays the current movie and all its scenes in a separate window. The movie loops until the window is closed.
>
> **Test Scene** plays only the current scene in a separate window. The scene loops until the window is closed.
>
> **Loop Playback** is an option. When selected, the Play command loops repeatedly.
>
> **Play All Scenes** is an option. When selected, the Play command plays through all scenes of the current movie.
>
> **Enable Frame Actions** is an option. When selected, the Play command executes any frame actions in the movie.
>
> **Enable Buttons** is an option. When selected, buttons are active and will display their states in response to the mouse actions. The buttons will be active whether or not the movie is playing.

**Enable Sounds** is an option. When selected, the Play command will execute any sounds embedded in the movie.

## DRAWING

**Curves** can be drawn with the Pencil tool set in either Smooth or Ink Pencil Mode. Curves can also be added to existing lines using the Arrow tool.

**Lines** can be drawn with the Line tool.

**Ovals** can be drawn with the Oval tool.

**Rectangles** can be drawn with the Rectangle tool.

## DROPPER

The Dropper tool is used to determine the fill or line style of any graphic. When clicked on a fill, the settings used for that fill are selected by default for the Paint Bucket and Brush tools. When used on a line, the settings for that line are selected by default for the Pencil and Line tools.

## ERASER

The Eraser tool is used to erase portions of images. The Eraser controls include:

**Eraser Mode** controls what can be painted on. Erase Normal applies the eraser anywhere. Erase Fills erases only fills, leaving lines alone. Erase Line erases lines only, leaving fills alone. Erase Selected Fills applies the eraser to selected fills only. Erase Inside erases only the inside fill where you begin painting.

The **Faucet** option deletes an entire fill area or line segment.

**Eraser Shape** is used to set the size and shape of the eraser.

## FILLS

**Gradient fills** are area fills consisting of more than one color. They can be created by accessing the Color dialog box from the palette of any of the line, shape, or fill tools. Click on the Gradient tab. The two types of gradient fills are linear and radial. Both types can contain from two to eight colors. Individual colors can also be set to transparent using the Alpha slider (see Figure A–2).

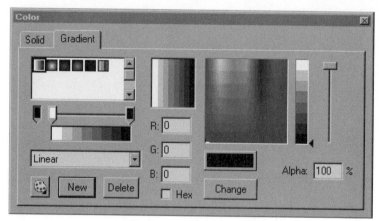

**FIGURE A–2** The Color dialog box with Gradient tab selected

**Solid fills** are area fills consisting of colors of varying transparency. Accessing the palette or Color dialog box from the palette of any of the line, shape, or fill tools can change the fill color. Click on the Solid tab. Colors can be set to levels of transparency using the Alpha slider.

### FRAMES

Frames are still images, displayed for discrete moments in time for each layer. Animation in Flash consists of each frame being shown in order. The speed at which the frames are displayed is controlled by the frames per second (fps) setting in Flash. A setting of 12 fps, which is the default setting, means that 12 frames will be displayed every second. The fps setting can be changed using the Movie Properties dialog box.

### GRID

The grid consists of horizontal and vertical lines useful for placing graphic elements during development. The distance between the grid lines can be changed using the Movie Properties dialog box. The Snap option causes graphic elements to align themselves along grid lines automatically when they are created, modified, or moved. The grid view can be toggled using the menu option View→Grid.

## GROUP

Several graphic objects can be combined together using the Group command. To use it, select more than one object and choose Modify→Group. When objects are grouped, they can be moved, resized, and rotated at the same time. They maintain their integrity, and can be Ungrouped.

## HAND

The Hand tool moves the viewing area. It has no effect on graphic elements.

## IMPORT

The menu option File→Import places a graphic or sound file in the current movie's library. It can then be added to the movie.

## INK BOTTLE

To change an existing line's color, size, and style, use the Ink Bottle tool. To change multiple different lines at once, select them all and use the Ink Bottle. The settings on the Ink Bottle are Line Color, Line Size, and Line Style.

## INSTANCE PROPERTIES

Instance properties are used to modify symbols at specific keyframes. The Instance Property dialog box can be accessed by selecting a specific symbol at a keyframe and choosing Modify→ Instance. The Color Effect tab can be used to change the color or transparency of the symbol at that keyframe. The Definition tab specifies a label name for the instance as well as its behavior at that keyframe. If it is an animated symbol, this dialog box also controls looping behavior (see Figure A–3).

## KEYFRAMES

Keyframes are special types of frames where actions or animation changes can be set. They serve as placeholders on the Timeline where any symbol's animated behavior changes, starts, or stops. Frames, which are static, mark continuing motion between keyframes. Changes or actions cannot be set in a frame that is not a keyframe. When you create frame-by-frame animation, every frame is a keyframe. In tweened animation, you define keyframes

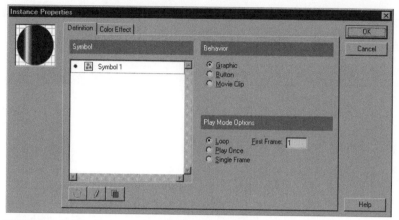

**FIGURE A–3** The Instance Properties dialog box

at important points in the animation and let Flash control the content of frames between those points. Keyframes exist in specific layers and can be created by selecting a layer and a specific frame and choosing Insert→Keyframe.

## LASSO

The Lasso tool is used to select portions of a graphic element rather than the entire thing. The Magic Wand modifier can be used to select colors in a particular area. The color at the first point that you click with the Magic Wand, as well as all other colors that fall within the specified tolerance, are ignored. All other colors in the Lasso area are selected. You can modify the color tolerance with the Magic Wand Properties button. The Polygon option makes the Lasso draw straight lines.

## LAYERS

Layers are used to separate graphic objects and symbols, to allow more control. The currently selected layer has a black label with white text and a pencil icon to the right of its name. Only one symbol in a layer may be animated, so multiple animated symbols require multiple layers. Each layer can contain keyframes at different locations. To create a layer, choose the menu option Insert→Layer. To rename a layer, double-click on its name. There is also a special type of layer called a Motion Guide, used for creating animation paths for symbols to follow (see Figure A–4).

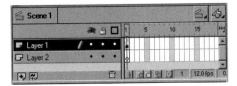

**FIGURE A–4** Layers

## LAYER VIEWS

When you deal with more than one layer, it is possible to hide, lock, and view outlines of the other layers. Hiding the other layers leaves only one layer's contents visible on the scene. Locking the other layers leaves all the other contents visible, but not editable. Viewing outlines converts all the graphics in a particular layer to outlines of a single color. To hide or lock layers, click under the eye icon or the lock icon. The outlines can be turned on by clicking under the small square next to the lock icon. Also, the Layer menu can be used. The Layer menu is accessible by right-clicking (PC) or Ctrl-clicking (Mac) on a layer.

## LIBRARIES

The Libraries menu item contains already created buttons, sounds, symbols, components, and movie clips from Macromedia.

## LIBRARY

The Library dialog box contains all the symbols in a movie. Instances of symbols can be dragged from this dialog box on to the current scene. The Library contains graphic symbols, sounds, and imported images (see Figure A–5).

## LINE TOOL

The Line tool is used to draw straight lines. The settings on the Line tool are Line Color, Line Size, and Line Style.

## MAGNIFIER

The Magnifier tool is used to zoom the view of the scene in and out. This is also controlled by the Zoom drop-down box on the top toolbar. The two modifiers are Enlarge and Reduce. When the view is reduced, the zoomed-in scene is centered at the spot on the scene where the Magnifier was clicked.

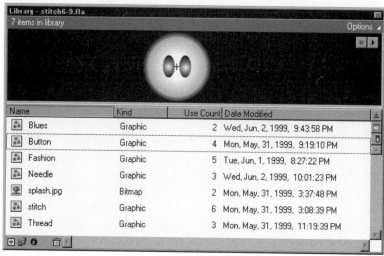

**FIGURE A–5** The Library dialog box

## MOVIE PROPERTIES

The Movie Properties dialog box can be opened by choosing Modify→ Movie (see Figure A–6).

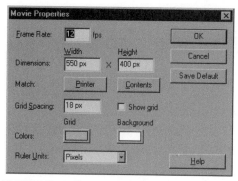

**FIGURE A–6** The Movie Properties dialog box

**Frame Rate** controls how many frames per second are played when the movie is viewed.

**Dimensions** are the width and height of the movie in pixels. The units can be changed using the Ruler Units drop-down menu at the bottom of this dialog box.

The **Match Printer** and **Contents** buttons set the movie dimensions based on the printer settings or the contents of the movie.

**Grid Spacing** sets the number of pixels between grid lines. Show grid displays the grid just like View→Grid.

**Grid** and **Background Colors** can be changed with the Colors buttons.

## MOVIES

Movies in Flash consist of all the keyframes, actions, sounds, layers, and scenes located together in the same .fla file.

## ONION SKINS

The Onion Skins setting displays multiple frames of an animation at the same time. The Onion Skin button is directly beneath the Timeline under all the layers. The Onion Skin Outline button displays the multiple frames as outlines. When either of the two buttons are selected, the Onion Skin Markers appear on the Timeline and can be moved to set the beginning and ending of the displayed sequence (see Figure A–7).

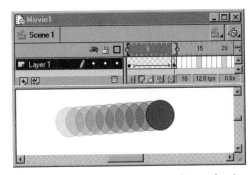

**FIGURE A–7** The Onion Skin outlines of animated circle

## OUTLINES

The View Outlines command displays all the graphics on the scene as outlines.

## OVAL TOOL

The Oval tool is used to draw circles and oval shapes. The settings for the oval include:

> **Line Color**, which can be set as any solid color with partial or full transparency
>
> **Line Thickness**
>
> **Line Style**
>
> **Fill Color**, which can be any solid or gradient fill with partial or full transparency

## PAINT BUCKET

The Paint Bucket is used to add or replace a current fill to a graphic object. The Gap Size drop-down box specifies what size gaps in an object's border are permissible for it to still be filled. The Paint Bucket can also be used to modify existing gradient fills using the Transform Fill option. The Lock Fill option allows you to extend the same gradient fill across multiple filled objects.

## PUBLISH

The menu option File→Publish uses the current Publish Settings and generates the appropriate files.

## PUBLISH PREVIEW

File→Publish Preview creates a temporary version of the current movie and opens a browser window to display it.

## PUBLISH SETTINGS

File→Publish Settings opens the Publish Settings dialog box. This dialog box is used to specify all the files and settings that should be created. The Formats tab displays a number of check boxes and file types that can be produced, as well as text boxes where they can be given specific names (see Figure A–8).

> The **Flash tab** controls Flash settings. Load Order is the order in which the layers of the movie are loaded. Generate size report produces a text file with information on all the pieces of the final Flash movie and their sizes. This is useful for figuring out how to optimize the movie. Protect from import keeps the movie file from being downloadable by

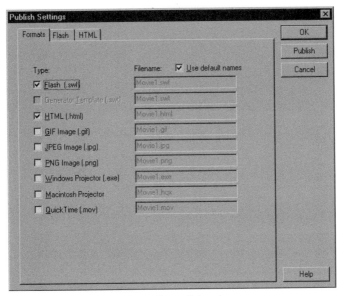

**FIGURE A–8** The Publish Settings dialog box

viewers. The JPEG Quality slider controls the amount of compression Flash uses on any imported images. Audio Stream and Audio Event Set buttons are used to change the streaming and event compressions used. Finally, the Version drop-down is used to specify which version of Flash to create. If Flash 3 is used, any Flash 4 features in the movie will not function (see Figure A–9).

The **HTML tab** controls how Flash creates HTML files. The Template drop-down contains a variety of precreated HTML templates into which Flash can embed the movie. The Dimensions setting specifies the size at which the movie will be displayed. Setting this to Percent will cause the movie to scale to fit the browser. The other options control how the movie will display, where on the page it will reside, and what menu options will be available to the viewer who right-clicks (PC) or Ctrl-clicks (Mac) on the movie (see Figure A–10).

## RECTANGLE TOOL

The Rectangle tool is used to draw squares and rectangle shapes. The settings for the rectangle include:

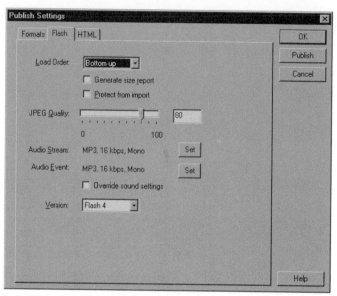

**FIGURE A–9** The Publish Settings dialog box with Flash tab selected

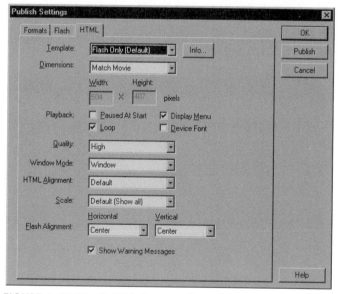

**FIGURE A–10** The Publish Settings dialog box with HTML tab selected

**Line Color**, which can be set as any solid color with partial or full transparency

**Line Thickness**

**Line Style**

**Fill Color**, which can be any solid or gradient fill with partial or full transparency

**Round Rectangle Radius**, which is used to give the rectangle rounded corners

## ROTATE

The Arrow tool and the Rotate modifier can be used on any selected object. When the Rotate option is on, the selected object displays small handles that can be clicked and dragged to rotate the object (see Figure A–11).

**FIGURE A–11** Rotate cursor

## SCALE

The Arrow tool and the Scale modifier can be used on any selected object. When the Scale option is on, the selected object displays small handles that can be clicked and dragged to scale the object (see Figure A–12).

**FIGURE A–12** Scale cursor

## SCENES

Scenes in Flash consist of keyframes, actions, sounds, and layers. A movie may contain multiple scenes.

## SELECTING

Graphic objects must be selected to be modified or moved. The Arrow tool is used to select objects. Selected objects are indicated by a crosshatch or checkerboard pattern. Multiple objects can be selected by using the Arrow and clicking and dragging a selection box around them, or using the Arrow and the Shift key.

## SHAPE HINTS

Shape Hints are used to help control shape tweening. To add Shape Hints, you must first have created a shape tweened animation. Clicking on the shape at the first keyframe allows the selection of Modify→Transform→Add Shape Hints. A small circle with a letter appears at either end of the animation. The beginning area this circle is placed on will match the final location of the letter at the last keyframe (see Figure A–13).

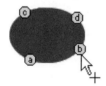

**FIGURE A–13** Shape Hints

## SMOOTH

To increase the smoothness of a line, the menu option Modify→ Curves→Smooth can be used. The Arrow tool has a Smooth button that does the same thing.

## SOUNDS

Flash 4 supports WAV, AIFF, and mp3 sound file types. To use a sound file, it must first be imported using the File→Import command. Once imported, it can be dragged from the Library window to keyframes in the main movie or keyframes of buttons.

## STRAIGHTEN

To increase the straightness of a line, the menu option Modify→ Curves→Straighten can be used. The Arrow tool also has a Straighten button that does the same thing.

## SYMBOLS

Flash symbols are graphic objects that are stored by Flash. They are important because they can be reused. When you create a symbol, you can use it over and over again without having to redraw it each time you need it. If you decide to change it, you don't need to change each instance (copy) of it; you can simply change the stored master symbol. Changing the master symbol changes all the instances of it in your Flash movie.

There are three types of symbols: graphics, buttons, and movie clips. Graphics are images that can have animation and sounds attached. They are noninteractive. Buttons are graphics that can also respond to mouse actions. Movie clips are entire Flash movies that can be reused inside another movie.

## SYMBOLS, CREATING

There are two ways to create a symbol. After you have created a graphic you want to convert, you can either choose the menu option Insert→Create Symbol or press the F8 key. Once you have created the symbol, it is automatically stored in the local Library.

## SYMBOLS, EDITING

There are several ways to edit symbols. In the Library, you can select the symbol you wish to edit and pull up the Symbol menu by clicking on the Options button on the top right. You can also choose Edit→Edit Symbols. Once you are in symbol editing mode, you can switch between symbols by using the Symbol List button at the top-right side of the window (see Figure A–14).

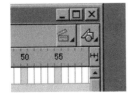

**FIGURE A–14** The Symbol List button

## TEXT TOOL

The Text tool is used to draw text objects. The settings for the rect-angle include:

**Font**
**Font Size**
**Font Color**
**Bold** and **Italic** styles
**Alignment**
**Paragraph Properties**
**Text Input modifier.** With this set, the Text tool creates input boxes.

## TIMELINE

The Timeline is at the top of the Flash movie editor. The purpose of the Timeline is to serve as a placeholder for the frames in the animation. Using the Timeline menu immediately to the right can modify the view of the Timeline. The Preview and Preview in Context options display thumbnail versions of the graphic objects instead of frames.

## TWEENING

Tweening is the process Flash uses to create animation between keyframes by interpolating the intermediate frames. Flash pro-vides a time-saving method of animation that requires only the creation of the most important frames. In using tweening, key-frames serve as turning points during an animation, and Flash fills in the gaps.

## TWEENING, MOTION

Motion tweening consists of giving an object a starting and an ending location and letting Flash interpolate the frames between them. Motion tweening also interpolates based on object size and rotation.

## TWEENING, SHAPE

Shape tweening animation is used when you need to change or morph one shape into another. The shape and the color shifts gradually from the beginning graphic to the final one. As in motion tweening, Flash will interpolate the intermediate frames.

## UNGROUP

Modify→Ungroup is used to return objects grouped together using the Group command to their original distinct states.

## ZOOM

The Zoom drop-down box is used to zoom the view of the scene in and out. The values in the drop-down box can be selected, and percentages can also be typed into the box. Zoom is also controlled by the Magnifier tool.

# Index

## A

Action
    adding, 210–211
    application. *See* Buttons.
    code, adding, 111–113
    layer, modifying, 176–179
    setting. *See* Keyframes.
    stopping. *See* Menu scene animation.
Action to Get URL, 205
Actions
    layer, 109–111
    tab, 176–178, 182, 185, 204, 210, 220, 221,
        223, 227, 228
Address Sphere, 38
Address Text, 45, 59
    animating, 55–57
    color, changing, 69–70
    layer, 18, 19, 36, 56
ADPCM, 97
AIFF file, 86, 172, 173
Align/Alignment button, 15, 18
Align dialog box, 217
Alpha
    changes, 194
    choice, 66, 68, 194
    slider, 156
    sliding, 158, 159, 162–164, 168
    value, 36, 143, 155
Animated buttons, 187–191
Animation, 45–46, 54, 55, 73, 89, 107, 147, 190

action stopping. *See* Menu scene.
    adding, 146, 194
    creating. *See* Preloading.
    effects, 152
    frames, 100
    steps, 204
    viewing, 151
Antialiased graphics, 209
Antialiasing, 13. *See also* Text.
Apache, 118
Applet. *See* Java applets.
    HTML code, 94
Arrow tool, 3, 8, 12, 13, 122, 145, 154, 169
    change, 127, 30–32, 49, 125, 137, 139
    dragging, 27
    selection, 23, 150
    usage, 15, 16, 18, 42, 43, 53, 62, 128, 167,
        177, 207, 227, 228. *See also* Text.
Audio Stream, 97
AVI, 94

## B

Background, 45, 51, 54, 134, 209
    animation, 146
    change, 172
    fill, creating, 29–34
    layer, adding, 44
    music, 172–186
Background color, 103, 206
    change, 115

Background curve
    animating, 48–51
    creating, 27–29
Behavior setting, 223
Behavior to Label, 181
BMP, 40
Browsers, 115, 211
Brush Mode, Paint Normal, 140
Brush tool, 4, 140
    effects, 140–146
Button actions, 79–85, 206
    application, 219–222, 224–226
    keyframes, adding, 80
    testing, 85
Button animation, 155
    testing, 156
Button frame actions, 76
    window, opening, 79
Button images, 189
    moving, 153–156
Button layer, 131, 148, 153, 177, 186, 199
Button over state, movie clip addition, 190–191
Button Shadow, 148
    creating, 140–142
    layer, 149, 151, 190
Button sounds, 86
    adding, 87–88
Button Symbol, 189
    creating, 148–149
    layer, 149
    motion, adding, 198
    selection, 154
Buttonholes
    creating, 132–134
    thread fill, adding, 134–135
Buttons. See Animated buttons.
    adding, 216–218, 227–230
    animating, 147, 149–151
    creating, 74–78, 173–175. See also Parent buttons.
    inserting. See Link buttons; Movies.
    self-animation, 148
    texture, creating, 130–132
    Web links, adding, 77–78

C
Circles
    connecting, lines usage, 25–27
    creating, 21–22. See also Transparent circle.
    duplicate movement, 22–25
    duplicating, 22–25
    fills, changing, 34–35
    layers, creating, 44–45
    modifying. See Transparent circle.

Clips
    adding. See Movie clips; Splash screen.
    creating. See Movie clips.
Color
    button, 130
    change, 212. See also Address text.
    dialog box, 30, 126, 131, 134, 142, 143
    hue effects, 170
    markers, 130, 131
    palette, 60, 136
    values, change, 67, 69
Color Edit, 82, 84
    button, 130
Color Effect, 66, 68
    tab, 158, 159, 162–164, 168, 171, 194
Compression, 97
Contact form, 121
Content Type, 119
Curves, animating/creating. See Background curve.

D
Definition tab, 219, 224
Down frame, creating, 83–85
Down keyframe, 189
Drawing toolbar, 2–4
Dropper, 4

E
Easing slider, 61
Editing screen, 174
Effects, 187
EMBED tag, 103
Embedded movie. See HyperText Markup Language.
Eraser, 4
Export Flash Player dialog box, 184

F
Fading, 64–70
File preferences, 8
File Transfer Protocol (FTP), 106
File Type
    dialog box, 119
    usage, choice, 94
Fill Color, 22, 84
    button, 29, 30, 126
Fills. See Gradients.
    changing. See Circles.
    creating. See Background fill.
Flash 4
    Active X control, 103
    basics, 1
    detection, movie modification, 115–117

files, 94, 230
form, 205–206
format, 100
introduction, 2
movie, 118
player, 103
settings, choice, 96–97
site, 115
symbols, 71
version usage, choice, 94
Flash-based menuing system, 121
Flash plug-in, 93, 118
    detection, 119
Fonts, 11, 109
    choice, 173
    outline options, 209
    selection, 207
    sizes, 7, 135, 136
    styles, 7
Format settings, choice, 94–95
Forms, 205–211. *See also* Flash 4.
    controls, 208
    creating, 206–208
Frame-by-frame animation, 149
Frame Properties
    dialog box, 50–51, 54, 88, 176, 181, 201
Frame Rate, 4
Frames, 41–48
    calling, 215
    copying, 192–193
    creating. *See* Down frame; Hit frame; Over
        frame.
    option, 112
Freehand graphics, 140

**G**

Generate Size Report button, 96
GET, usage, 211
Get URL, choice, 115, 210, 211
GIF, 2, 40, 94. *See also* Static GIF.
    images, 104
Gradient fill, 138, 145
Gradients, 82, 84
    creating. *See* Shadow gradient.
    modifying. *See* Shadow gradient.
    tab, 126, 130, 134
Graphic objects, 8, 71
Graphics, 72, 107, 152, 164, 192
    drawing, 123–126, 128–129
    importing, 38–39
    program, 139
    reshaping, 122

selection, 8
starting, 122–123
tilting, 127–128
Grids
    color, changing, 124
    options, 217
    spacing, 122
    visibility, 123

**H**

Header layer, 17
Header Text, 15, 45
    animating, 58–59
    layer, 10, 58, 60, 113
Hints, adding. *See* Shapes.
Hit frame, creating, 81–82
HyperText Markup Language (HTML)
    boxes, 95
    code, 102. *See also* Applet.
    creation, 101, 211
    embedded movie, 117
    file, 106, 230
    option, choice, 99
    reference, 102
    settings, choice, 97–99
    tab, 97, 104, 119
    tags, 102
    uploading, 114
    writing. *See* .swf file.

**I**

IIS 4.0, configuring, 118–119
Images, 224
    adding, 139–140
    fading, 156–157, 194
    importing, 38
    resizing, 195–198
Input boxes, 207
Insert Layer, 27
    choice, 44
Instance, dragging, 219
Instance Properties, 54, 64, 75–76, 78, 155, 159,
        162, 163, 177
    dialog box, 219
Interactive activity, 211–230
    starting, 212–213
Interactivity, 119, 186. *See also* Pages.
Internet Explorer, 5, 93
Internet Information Server, 119
Internet Service Provider (ISP), 118
Intersections, 129–140

## J

Java applets, 106
Java files, 106
JavaScript, usage, 114
JPEG, 2, 40, 96
    compression, 230
    Data box, 38
    quality, 101

## K

Keyframes, 46–50, 52–59, 62–69, 74, 150, 179, 193
    actions, setting, 222–223, 226–227
    adding. *See* Button actions; Pages.
    changing, 217, 218
    creation, 199
    images, 160, 164
    inserting, 83, 110, 151, 153, 154, 162, 166,
        168, 171, 173, 176, 177, 181–183, 199,
        204, 215, 223, 229
    movie clip, creating, 223–224
    position, 64
    returning, 216
    selection, 83, 109, 111, 113, 155–157, 160,
        163, 167, 176, 198, 200–202, 204, 210,
        218, 224

## L

Labels
    adding. *See* Text.
    layer, 180
    radio button, 222, 225
    tab, 216, 226
Lasso tool, 3
Layer menu, 33, 48, 51, 54, 57, 135, 137, 153,
    193, 202
    option, 166
Layers
    adding, 175
    creating, 10. *See also* Circles.
    dragging, 171
Leave Protect From Import, 96
Library, 72, 174
    dialog box, 38, 79, 176, 189, 213, 219
    image, dragging, 199
    sounds, adding, 86
Line Color, 21, 25
    transparency, 131
Line segment, 28
Line tool, 3, 6, 25, 166
Link buttons, inserting, 198–202
Link Circle, 23, 34, 87
    instances, 75

Link hand cursor, 78
Link spheres, 77, 79, 81
    animating, 51–55
    fading, 68–69
    instance properties, changing, 75–76
    selection, 54
    symbols, 79, 83
Link Text, 45
    layer, 17, 19, 57
    symbol, creating, 42
Links
    animating, 57–58
    Layer, 198, 199, 201
    testing, 78
Load Order, 96
Logo, 45
    image, 22
    layer, 42–44, 66
    lines, fading, 66–67
Loops, 180
Lynx, usage, 93

## M

Macintoshes, 93
Macromedia, 93
    libraries, 72
    Sound Library, usage, 86–87, 88
Magnifier, 4
Match Movie, dimensions, 97
Menu page, creation, 205
Menu scene, 192
    animation, action stopping, 204–205
Menuing systems, 186
Motion
    layer, 165–168
    option, 155
    smoothness, 46
Motion Guide, 165, 166
Motion tweening, 59, 69, 169
    adding, 170, 171
Mouse
    actions, 85
    clicks, link, 81
    pointer, 131
Movement. *See* Needles.
    tweening, 48–59
Movie animation, 151
Movie clips, 187, 215, 223
    adding, 180–185. *See also* Button over state.
    creating, 175, 189–190, 215–216. *See also*
        Keyframes.
Movie file, 230
Movie instance, 224

Movie properties, 4–5, 27
  dialog box, 45, 115
Movies
  buttons, inserting, 176
  creating, 172–173
  HTML page, creating, 117–118
  modification. *See* Flash.
  optimizing, 101–102
  publishing, 99
  scenes, adding, 107–108
  size, 206, 212
  testing, 229
mp3 file, 173
Multipurpose Internet Mail Extension (MIME)
  type, 118, 119
Music. *See* Background music.
  layer, adding, 179–180
  movie, 180

**N**

Needle layer, selection, 168
Needles, 195
  drawing, 123–126
  fading, 168–169
  growth, 192
  lines, 129
  movement, 168–169
  rotation, 168–169
  texture, filling, 126–127
  tilting, 127–128
Netscape Navigator, 93
Non-Flash version. *See* Web site.
  creating. *See* Pages.
Noninteractive images, 72
Nontext graphic, 138

**O**

Object Inspector, 19, 20, 60, 189
  opening, 48, 58, 124, 195, 213
  settings, 158, 160
  usage, 131, 157, 162, 165
Objects, onion-skinned path, 55, 57, 58
Office Photo, 45
  fading, 65–66
  layer, 65
On MouseEvent, 178
  choice, 210, 227, 228
  selection, 220, 224
Onion Skin Markers, 51
Onion-skinning, 48, 51
Opening sequences, 152–172
  starting, 153

Outline, 125
  options, 209
Oval tool, 3, 4, 6
  change, 124
  usage, 131, 133
Over frame
  creating, 82–83
  label, 173
Over keyframes, 175
Over state, 187

**P**

Pages. *See* Web pages.
  animating, 41
  animation, 59
  Flash version, creation, 9
  interactivity, 70, 71
  layout, keyframe adding, 47–48
  links, 16
  non-Flash version, creating, 103–106
  section, 100
Paint Bucket, 30, 31, 34, 35, 82, 142
  change, 36, 60, 139
  choice, 126, 134
  selection, 130
  usage, 83, 84, 127, 143
Palette, 29
  box, 11
  button, 37
PARAM tag, 103
Parameters, 177, 178
Parent buttons, 190, 199
  creating, 188–189
  dragging, 217
  finding, 216
Parent symbol, 190
Pencil
  Mode, 128
  setting, 128
  tool, 4
Photo, 194, 215
  layer, 139, 171
  settings, changing, 38–39
  symbols, 65
Photographs
  adding, 139–140, 202–204
  fade-in, 171–172
  shadow creation, 140–142
Platform usage, choice, 93–94
Playback boxes, 98
Plug-in, detecting, 114–118
Preload scenes, modifying, 108–109
Preloader, 111

Preloading, 107–114
  animation, creating, 109–111
Press check boxes, 221, 225
Products layer, 53
  keyframe, 76
Products Sphere layer, 51
Publish Settings, 230
  dialog box, 95–97
  selection, 99
Publishing, 91, 94–106, 230
Push button, 208

**R**

Radial Fill, 82, 84
Raster graphics, 2, 101
Rectangle tool, 3, 4, 6, 29, 206
Release check boxes, 221, 225, 227, 228
Reshaping, 121–129
Resolution, choice, 92–93
RGB
  changes, 25, 34, 82, 84
  setting, 30
  usage, 136
  values, 11, 126, 131
Rotate
  button, 142, 150
  option, 128
  settings, usage, 169
Rotation, 145, 148, 156
  movie clip, 190
  symbol, 190
Round Rectangle Radius button, 6–7

**S**

S shape
  creating, 26, 59–61
  shape tweening, applying, 61–62
Scale
  button, 13, 32, 142
  option, 37, 60, 202
  settings, usage, 169
Scene editing mode, 152
Scene Inspector, 107, 191
Scene List button, 107, 113, 192, 210
Scenes
  adding. *See* Movies.
  animation, action stopping. *See* Menu scene
      animation.
  creating, 191–192, 210
  modifying. *See* Preload scenes.
Shadow gradient
  creating, 142–143
  modifying, 143–146

Shadow graphic, deletion, 170
Shadow shape, drawing, 140
Shadows, 194
  creating, 140–142
  deselection, 142
  layer, 140, 145
  movement/shape/tint. *See* Text.
  repositioning/selection, 148
  text, creating, 14–16
Shape drawing, 3, 6–7, 20–34
Shape tweening, 59–64
Shapes. *See* Brush shapes.
  drawing. *See* Shadow shape.
  hints, adding, 62–64
  making, 130
  modification, 20–34
Shockwave Flash, 94
Show Warning Messages box, 99
Size report, viewing, 99–101
Snap
  button, 12, 24, 26, 125, 150
  options, 217
Sound effects, 86–89
Sounds
  adding. *See* Button sounds; Library.
  layer, 87
  library, 88
  tab, 179
Source code, 117
Spheres, 45
  animating. *See* Link spheres.
  layers, 37, 52, 59, 61
  linking, 77
  shape, 134
Splash movie, 172, 185
Splash scene, 192
  animation, 204
Splash screen, 122, 147, 153, 155, 173, 193
  animation, 172
  clips addition, 185–186
  size, 186
Splash sequence, 148
Static elements, adding, 213–215
Static GIF, 103, 104
Static graphic, 187
Stop action
  adding, 210
  putting, 113–114
.swf file, HTML writing, 102–103
Symbol editing, 72–73
  mode, 73, 83, 149
  screen, 188
Symbol library, 72, 188
Symbol List button, 189

Symbol properties, 23, 35, 74, 79
Symbols, 65, 71–74, 174, 175
    access, Library usage, 72
    animating, 147–152
    creating, 72, 152. *See also* Button Symbol.
    editing window, 79
    menus, 72
    types, changing, 74
    usage, 147

**T**

Tags layers, 110
Target, 222
Tell Target, 221, 223, 225, 226
Text
    animation, 55–59, 157–165
    antialiasing, 212
    area, 209
    boxes, variable setting, 209
    coloring, 138–139
    creating, 6–7, 135–138
    drawing/modification, 9–20
    fading, 157–165
    labels, 218–219
    layer, 10, 138, 157, 165
    linking, 16–19
    links, 57–58, 67–68
    location, 213
    motion guide, 193
    moving, 19–20
    objects, 19
    properties, setting, 11–12
    resizing, 137
    selection, arrow tool usage, 229
    shadow, movement/shape/tint, 169–171
    symbol, creating. *See* Link text symbol.
    tool, 7, 11, 60, 135, 173, 175, 199, 202, 207
Text Color button, 15
Text Input Box, 207, 209
Texture, 143
    creating, 34. *See also* Buttons.
    filling, 34–38, 126–127
Threads, 128–129, 217
    dragging, 204
    fading, 156–157
    fill, adding. *See* Buttonholes.
    layer, 128
    lengthening, 192, 204
    lines, 129
    moving, 195
    selection, 137
    symbol, 214

Tilting. *See* Graphics; Needles.
Timelines, 41–48
Tint
    Amount, 217
    choice, 67, 69, 217
Transform Fill, 143
Transitions, 191–205
Transparency, 34–38. *See also* Line Color.
    adding, 170
Transparent circle, creating/modifying, 36–38
Turn Off Music graphic, 177
Turn On Music graphic, 178
Tween Scaling, 50, 54, 56, 58, 59, 64, 66
Tweening, 46, 56, 61, 64, 66, 147, 156
    adding, 110
    property, 160, 165
    setting, 157
    tab, 160, 169, 201
    type, 155

**U**

Undo Levels, 7–8
Unix machines, 93
Up frames, 84
Up keyframes, 175, 189
URLs, 78, 115, 185, 229
Use Default Names box, 95, 116

**V**

Variables, 209, 211
Vector graphics, 2

**W**

WAV file, 86, 172, 173
Web links, adding. *See* Buttons.
Web pages, 92, 94
Web publishing, 91, 106
Web server, 94, 118–119
Web site, non-Flash version, 114
Window Library, 174
Window list box, 115
Window Mode, 99
Windows, 93

**Z**

Zoom
    control, 15
    drop-down box, 49
    features, 5–6
    list box, 31

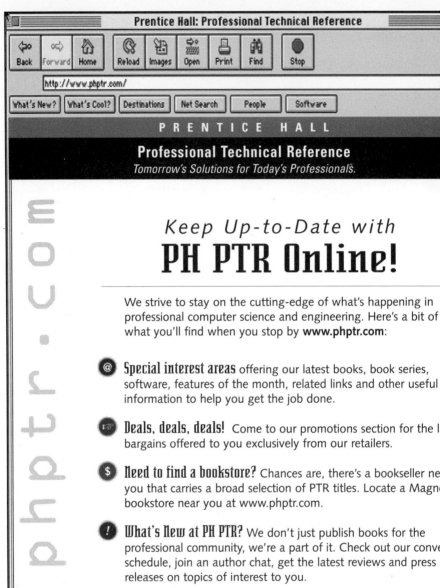